WORLD
HISTORY SERIES

The Civil War

Titles in the World History Series

WORLD HISTORY SERIES

The Civil War

by
James A. Corrick

LUCENT
BOOKS®

THOMSON
GALE

San Diego • Detroit • New York • San Francisco • Cleveland • New Haven, Conn. • Waterville, Maine • London • Munich

THOMSON
★
™
GALE

For the Corricks of Corrick's Ford.

© 2003 by Lucent Books. Lucent Books is an imprint of The Gale Group, Inc.,
a division of Thomson Learning, Inc.

Lucent Books® and Thomson Learning™ are trademarks used herein under license.

For more information, contact
Lucent Books
27500 Drake Rd.
Farmington Hills, MI 48331-3535
Or you can visit our Internet site at http://www.gale.com

LIBRARY OF CONGRESS CATALOGING-IN-PUBLICATION DATA

Corrick, James A.
    The Civil War / by James A. Corrick.
        p. cm. — (World history series)
Includes bibliographical references (p.) and index.
Contents: The great conflict—The road to war—1861, opening shots—1862, the eastern
war—1862, the western war—1863, the home fronts—1863, turning points—1864, the
war continues—1865, victory and defeat—War's aftermath.
    ISBN 1-59018-181-6 (hardback: alk. paper)
    1. United States—History—Civil War, 1861–1865—Juvenile literature.   [1. United
States—History—Civil War, 1861–1865.]   I. Title.   II. Series.
    E468.C78 2003
    973.7—dc21
                                                                    2002012562

Printed in the United States of America

Contents

Foreword

Each year on the first day of school, nearly every history teacher faces the task of explaining why his or her students should study history. One logical answer to this question is that exploring what happened in our past explains how the things we often take for granted—our customs, ideas, and institutions—came to be. As statesman and historian Winston Churchill put it, "Every nation or group of nations has its own tale to tell. Knowledge of the trials and struggles is necessary to all who would comprehend the problems, perils, challenges, and opportunities which confront us today." Thus, a study of history puts modern ideas and institutions in perspective. For example, though the founders of the United States were talented and creative thinkers, they clearly did not invent the concept of democracy. Instead, they adapted some democratic ideas that had originated in ancient Greece and with which the Romans, the British, and others had experimented. An exploration of these cultures, then, reveals their very real connection to us through institutions that continue to shape our daily lives.

Another reason often given for studying history is the idea that lessons exist in the past from which contemporary societies can benefit and learn. This idea, although controversial, has always been an intriguing one for historians. Those who agree that society can benefit from the past often quote philosopher George Santayana's famous statement, "Those who cannot remember the past are condemned to repeat it." Historians who subscribe to Santayana's philosophy believe that, for example, studying the events that led up to the major world wars or other significant historical events would allow society to chart a different and more favorable course in the future.

Just as difficult as convincing students to realize the importance of studying history is the search for useful and interesting supplementary materials that present historical events in a context that can be easily understood. The volumes in Lucent Books' World History Series attempt to present a broad, balanced, and penetrating view of the march of history. Ancient Egypt's important wars and rulers, for example, are presented against the rich and colorful backdrop of Egyptian religious, social, and cultural developments. The series engages the reader by enhancing historical events with these cultural contexts. For example, in *Ancient Greece,* the text covers the role of women in that society. Slavery is discussed in *The Roman Empire*, as well as how slaves earned their freedom. The numerous and varied aspects of everyday life in these and other societies are explored in each volume of the series. Additionally, the series covers the major political, cultural, and philosophical ideas as the torch of civilization is passed from ancient Mesopotamia and Egypt, through Greece, Rome, Medieval Europe, and other world cultures, to the modern day.

The material in the series is formatted in a thorough, precise, and organized manner. Each volume offers the reader a comprehensive and clearly written overview of an important historical event or period. The topic under discussion is placed in a broad, historical context. For example, *The Italian Renaissance* begins with a discussion of the High Middle Ages and the loss of central control that allowed certain Italian cities to develop artistically. The book ends by looking forward to the Reformation and interpreting the societal changes that grew out of the Renaissance. Thus, students are not only involved in an historical era, but also enveloped by the events leading up to that era and the events following it.

One important and unique feature in the World History Series is the primary and secondary source quotations that richly supplement each volume. These quotes are useful in a number of ways. First, they allow students access to sources they would not normally be exposed to because of the difficulty and obscurity of the original source. The quotations range from interesting anecdotes to farsighted cultural perspectives and are drawn from historical witnesses both past and present. Second, the quotes demonstrate how and where historians themselves derive their information on the past as they strive to reach a consensus on historical events. Lastly, all of the quotes are footnoted, familiarizing students with the citation process and allowing them to verify quotes and/or look up the original source if the quote piques their interest.

Finally, the books in the World History Series provide a detailed launching point for further research. Each book contains a bibliography specifically geared toward student research. A second, annotated bibliography introduces students to all the sources the author consulted when compiling the book. A chronology of important dates gives students an overview, at a glance, of the topic covered. Where applicable, a glossary of terms is included.

In short, the series is designed not only to acquaint readers with the basics of history, but also to make them aware that their lives are a part of an ongoing human saga. Perhaps they will then come to the same realization as famed historian Arnold Toynbee. In his monumental work, *A Study of History*, he wrote about becoming aware of history flowing through him in a mighty current, and of his own life "welling like a wave in the flow of this vast tide."

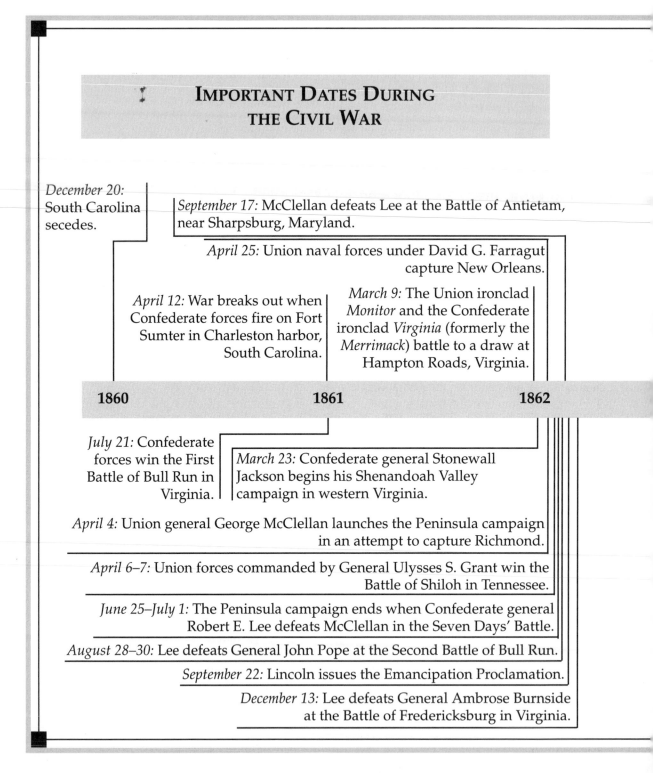

IMPORTANT DATES DURING THE CIVIL WAR

December 20: South Carolina secedes.

September 17: McClellan defeats Lee at the Battle of Antietam, near Sharpsburg, Maryland.

April 25: Union naval forces under David G. Farragut capture New Orleans.

April 12: War breaks out when Confederate forces fire on Fort Sumter in Charleston harbor, South Carolina.

March 9: The Union ironclad *Monitor* and the Confederate ironclad *Virginia* (formerly the *Merrimack*) battle to a draw at Hampton Roads, Virginia.

1860   **1861**   **1862**

July 21: Confederate forces win the First Battle of Bull Run in Virginia.

March 23: Confederate general Stonewall Jackson begins his Shenandoah Valley campaign in western Virginia.

April 4: Union general George McClellan launches the Peninsula campaign in an attempt to capture Richmond.

April 6–7: Union forces commanded by General Ulysses S. Grant win the Battle of Shiloh in Tennessee.

June 25–July 1: The Peninsula campaign ends when Confederate general Robert E. Lee defeats McClellan in the Seven Days' Battle.

August 28–30: Lee defeats General John Pope at the Second Battle of Bull Run.

September 22: Lincoln issues the Emancipation Proclamation.

December 13: Lee defeats General Ambrose Burnside at the Battle of Fredericksburg in Virginia.

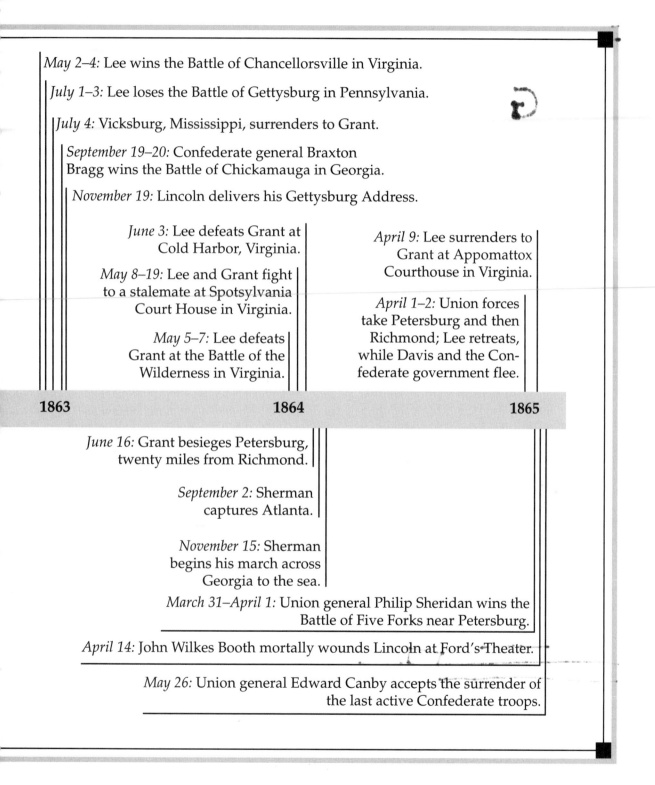

May 2–4: Lee wins the Battle of Chancellorsville in Virginia.

July 1–3: Lee loses the Battle of Gettysburg in Pennsylvania.

July 4: Vicksburg, Mississippi, surrenders to Grant.

September 19–20: Confederate general Braxton Bragg wins the Battle of Chickamauga in Georgia.

November 19: Lincoln delivers his Gettysburg Address.

June 3: Lee defeats Grant at Cold Harbor, Virginia.

May 8–19: Lee and Grant fight to a stalemate at Spotsylvania Court House in Virginia.

May 5–7: Lee defeats Grant at the Battle of the Wilderness in Virginia.

April 9: Lee surrenders to Grant at Appomattox Courthouse in Virginia.

April 1–2: Union forces take Petersburg and then Richmond; Lee retreats, while Davis and the Confederate government flee.

1863   **1864**   **1865**

June 16: Grant besieges Petersburg, twenty miles from Richmond.

September 2: Sherman captures Atlanta.

November 15: Sherman begins his march across Georgia to the sea.

March 31–April 1: Union general Philip Sheridan wins the Battle of Five Forks near Petersburg.

April 14: John Wilkes Booth mortally wounds Lincoln at Ford's Theater.

May 26: Union general Edward Canby accepts the surrender of the last active Confederate troops.

The Great Conflict

No event in United States history has captured the imagination of Americans as has the Civil War (1861–1865). Historian James M. McPherson observes:

> Five generations have passed, and that war is still with us. Hundreds of Civil War . . . and Lincoln Associations flourish today. Every year thousands of Americans dress up in blue and gray uniforms . . . to re-enact Civil War battles. . . . Popular and professional history magazines continue to chronicle every . . . aspect of the war. Hundreds of books about the conflict pour off the presses every year, adding to the more than 50,000 titles on the subject that make the Civil War by a large margin the most written-about event in American history.[1]

Part of this ongoing fascination comes from the Civil War's having been the largest and bloodiest war ever fought in the Western Hemisphere. It was war on an epic scale. Almost 3.5 million men served in the two armies. They fought in some 10,000 battles, skirmishes, raids, sieges, and naval actions. Their struggles surged across the southern half of the United States, from the Atlantic Ocean to Arizona, and reached northward into Pennsylvania and Ohio. Naval engagements took place all over the world.

This conflict was the first large-scale war to be fought with Industrial Age weapons. The Civil War saw the introduction of machine guns, repeating rifles, telescopic sights, and ironclad warships, as well as one submarine that actually sank an enemy vessel. Railroads for the first time played a major role in waging war, as trains carried troops and supplies, while the telegraph provided speedy communication. Other innovations included the use of balloons to direct artillery fire and the development of trench warfare.

NATIONAL DESTINY

Much of the fascination with the Civil War also comes from a recognition that the conflict was a pivotal event in American history. Indeed, the very fate of the United States was at the center of the contest. As McPherson notes, "the fate of slavery, the structure of society both North and South, . . . [and] the very survival of the United States . . . rested on the shoulders of those weary men in blue and gray who fought."[2] If the American Revolution created the United States, the American Civil War defined the nation.

Among other things, the Civil War swept away the old, prewar South, heavily dependent on farming, with little industry, dominated by an aristocratic elite. In its place would eventually grow a society like that of the North, an industrial culture, with broader opportunities for all of its citizens. And, with the end of the old South came the end of slavery in the United States. Before the war, millions of African Americans were slaves; afterward, all slaves were free.

Robert Smalls, a slave, was forced to work in the Confederate army during the Civil War.

STATE AND NATIONAL GOVERNMENT

Out of the Civil War also came a more unified country. Before the war, each state government believed that it, not the federal government, had supreme power within its own borders. The latter's major roles were to levy tariffs, which are taxes on imports; to finance and construct canals; and to maintain an army and navy for national defense.

In general, the policies that most affected the average citizen were those of the local community and, on a broader scale, the laws of a particular state. Indeed, states resisted any federal legislation that might extend federal power. They cited a principle called states' rights, which gave each state authority within its own borders, except for those powers that were reserved by the Constitution for the national government. States even claimed the right to secede, or leave the Union. As early as the War of 1812, several New England states contemplated secession if the country went to war with Great Britain.

The Civil War put an end to the notion that states were sovereign territories that could come and go as they pleased. The states were now units of a single country. And this unity is reflected in a change from the phrase "United States are" in the prewar years to the "United States is" in the postwar period. Thus, the federal government emerged as the central authority. Author Russell F. Weigley writes, "a changed direction was set. National systems of organizations . . . would increasingly predominate over the looser . . . bonds of unity that had preceded the great Civil War."[3]

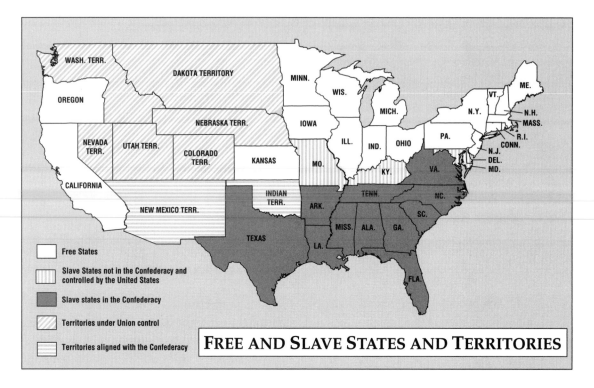

FREE AND SLAVE STATES AND TERRITORIES

THE PRICE OF WAR

Ending slavery, saving the United States, and creating a more unified nation came at a high human cost, for Civil War firepower was heavier, deadlier, and more accurate than in previous wars. Among the soldiers North and South, some 600,000 died; the death toll averaged more than 400 dead each day of the four-year struggle. Another 470,000 more were wounded, many of them losing arms and legs. Casualty rates were so great that even those who did not actually lose a husband, father, son, brother, or friend were horrified and sickened by the fate of so many young men. Scholar Robert Leckie observes that "it was a rare household that had not in some way suffered, and for decades the presence of limbless veterans on the streets of the towns and villages would remind Americans of . . . [their] sacrifice."[4]

In addition to the human loss was the widespread destruction in the South. At war's end, farms, homes, and cities lay in ruins. And as the South sought to build a new society on the wreckage of the old, poverty was everywhere, even among the once-wealthy plantation owners. But, in 1861, as the country began to split apart at the seams, these costs were still in the future.

1 The Road to War

The problems and issues that led to the Civil War were many and long-standing, and they all had their roots in the different ways of life found in the North and the South. As Weigley writes, "The Civil War armies were . . . ideological armies, waging war out of commitment to the beliefs and values of their respective societies."[5]

FARMS AND FACTORIES

The South was almost entirely a farming region, with few factories. Its main crops were cotton and tobacco, which were sold to the Northern states and Europe.

Although the North had widespread farming, it was also heavily industrialized. Indeed, much of the money Southern farmers earned from their crops went to buy farm equipment, clothing, and other manufactured goods from northern factories. The industrial economy of the North was able to support a much larger population than the rural South, 23 million Northerners as opposed to 9 million Southerners. According to historian Emory M. Thomas, "the South . . . had less than half as many people as the North, less than half the railroad mileage, less

than one-third the bank capital, and less than one-tenth the manufacturing output."[6]

SLAVERY

No issue divided the two sections, however, more than that of slavery. A third of the South's population consisted of some 3.5 million African Americans, almost all of whom were slaves. Most of these enslaved people labored on large farming estates, or plantations. Some acted as house servants, but the majority worked the fields, clearing, plowing, planting, and harvesting.

Slaves were expensive, and few whites in the South could afford them. Indeed, most of the estimated 350,000 slave owners had fewer than 5 slaves. Only 1,800 of them, all plantation holders, owned more than 100 slaves.

Still, most whites in the South favored slavery. Small farmers, as author Steven E. Woodworth observes,

considered it [slavery] a beneficial and indispensable feature of the great order of the universe. They fully approved of the South's "peculiar institution" and hoped to make it into the ranks of the slaveholders themselves

An African American man enslaved in the South stands with a bundle of cotton at his feet.

someday. They might well have relatives who were slaveholders and felt themselves connected to the slaveholding strata [class] of society by many ties, not the least of which was simply their common whiteness.[7]

Thus, those who did not own slaves dreamed of making enough money to buy a slave to help them raise more cash crops, the income from which might allow the purchase of more land and more slaves. Such an expansion could eventually lead to entry into the ranks of the plantation-owning elite, whose wealth made them the dominant political force in the South.

ABOLITIONISTS

The northern states did not have slavery, and although most Northerners shared the Southern belief that African Americans were inferior to whites, many also disliked slavery. Thus, it was in the North that vocal activists, known as abolitionists, banded together to seek the elimination of slavery.

Abolitionists were particularly active in resisting the spread of slavery west of the Mississippi River. Southerners were equally determined to see slavery in the West. Many Southerners feared that if slavery were banned from this region and portions of it entered as nonslaveholding or free states, the slave states would soon be outnumbered and lose political power. Indeed, if enough free states entered the Union, they might be able to declare slavery at an end in the United States.

COMPROMISING WITH SLAVERY

Neither pro- nor antislavery factions were able to dictate policy in the West. Rather a

Harriet Tubman, an abolitionist leader, helped to free many slaves through an escape network called the Underground Railroad.

series of congressional acts, beginning with the 1820 Missouri Compromise, tried to balance the interests of both sides. The Missouri Compromise allowed for the admission of slaveholding Missouri, which was part of the western territory bought from France in the 1803 Louisiana Purchase and which was settled mostly by Southerners. To maintain the free-slave balance, antislavery Maine was also admitted. Additionally, the Compromise split the remaining territory into slave and free, the dividing line running west from Missouri's southern border. North of that line, with the exception of Missouri, was free; any state south was slave.

In 1848, the Mexican War added new western land to the country. The slave-free balance was maintained by admitting Texas (slave) and California (free). But instead of extending the old boundary line westward, Congress decided in the Compromise of 1850 to allow the territorial legislatures to vote on whether to be slave or free.

In 1854, the Congress, upon the urging of Illinois senator Stephen A. Douglas, passed the Nebraska-Kansas Act, which revoked the Missouri Compromise. Although Douglas was against slavery, he wished to lure settlers into the Kansas and Nebraska Territories, which lay in the nonslave portion of the old Louisiana Purchase land. Douglas's hope was that the majority of the new settlers would be antislavery, as would any new states. His hope did not come true. Kansas, in particular, became a bloody battlefield, where anti- and proslavery supporters killed each other, sometimes individually and sometimes in pitched battles. It soon became known as Bleeding Kansas.

SOUTHERN ABOLITIONIST

There were Southerners who opposed slavery. Hinton R. Helper of North Carolina was one, as seen in this excerpt from his 1857 The Impending Crisis of the South:

"The causes which have impeded the progress and the prosperity of the South, which have dwindled our commerce, and other similar pursuits, into the most contemptible insignificance; sunk a large majority of our people in . . . poverty and ignorance, rendered a small minority conceited and tyrannical . . . ; entailed upon us a humiliating dependence on the Free States; disgraced us in the recesses of our own souls, and brought us under reproach from all civilized and enlightened nations— may all be traced to one common source . . . *Slavery!*

Reared amidst the institution of slavery, believing it to be wrong both in principle and in practice, and having seen and felt its evil influence upon individuals, communities and states, we [Helper] deem it a duty . . . to use our most strenuous efforts to overturn and abolish it! Then we are an abolitionist? Yes! . . . in the fullest sense of the term. We are not only in favor of keeping slavery out of the territories. . . . We here unhesitatingly declare ourself in favor of its immediate and unconditional abolition, in every state . . . where it now exists."

DRED SCOTT

As war raged in Kansas, a case landed in the Supreme Court that gave slave owners increased rights. In the 1840s, army surgeon John Emerson took his slave Dred Scott to various postings in non-slave parts of the United States. Eventually Scott was sent to Missouri, where Emerson's wife lived. There, he sued for his freedom on the basis of his having lived in the free Minnesota Territory.

After losing his suit in the Missouri state courts, Scott gained a hearing before the Supreme Court in 1857. Again, he lost. However, the court did not stop with Scott. The court expanded its ruling, decreeing that the federal government could not ban slavery in any part of the western territories, which meant that slavery could legally be spread to any part of the West.

JOHN BROWN

The Dred Scott decision enraged slavery opponents, enough so that many New

England towns held meetings to discuss the possible secession of their states. Another answer came from abolitionist John Brown. Brown's goal was to arm slaves and then carve out a free state in the mountains of Virginia and Maryland. Brown had been active in Kansas, where in response to an 1856 attack on Lawrence by proslavery raiders, he and some followers rode into slaveholding territory and kidnapped five men. Even though none of the men had had a hand in the Lawrence raid, Brown killed all five anyway.

Although short on recruits, both black and white, on October 16, 1859, Brown led a raid on the federal arsenal at Harpers Ferry, Virginia. His purpose was to seize weapons, but the raid failed, leaving six of the townspeople and ten of the attackers dead. Brown was captured, convicted of murder and treason, and hanged on December 2, 1859. To many Northerners, he was a hero, while to most Southerners, he was a villain.

ABRAHAM LINCOLN

While anti- and proslave factions clashed in Kansas and Virginia and in the courts, a new political party formed around abolition. With its platform demanding a West free from slavery, the Republican Party, which split from the older Whig Party in 1854, was a major force in the election of 1856, even though the presidential victor was the Democrat James Buchanan. The Republicans gained support throughout the remainder of the 1850s, and in November 1860, their candidate, Abraham Lincoln, was elected president.

Lincoln was born in 1809 in Kentucky and grew up on a farm in Indiana. The family had little money, and Lincoln spent far more time working the farm than he did going to school. He was to observe later that, in total, he spent no more than a year in the classroom. His education came from books that he borrowed from neighbors and friends.

When Lincoln was twenty-one, he moved with his family to Illinois, where over the next few years he worked as a fence maker, a crewman on a flatboat, a postmaster, and a surveyor. In 1832 he joined a company of volunteers to fight the Native American Sauk and Fox tribes in the Black Hawk War. Elected captain of his company, Lincoln saw no fighting,

Dred Scott sued for his freedom before the Supreme Court in 1857.

Federal troops enter the arsenal held by John Brown and his raiders at Harpers Ferry.

but the expedition gave him his only military experience.

Upon his discharge, Lincoln unsuccessfully sought election to the Illinois state legislature, finally winning a seat in 1834. Intent on preparing himself for his new job, he began studying law and, in 1836, passed the bar examination. He then moved to Springfield, the Illinois capital, and set up a law practice, which proved so successful it earned him a yearly income that often exceeded that of the state's governor.

In 1842, Lincoln married Mary Todd, with whom he would have four children, all sons; only one, Robert, reached adulthood. Five years later, Lincoln was elected to Congress, but lost reelection in 1848 because of his opposition to the popular Mexican War. Believing that his

political career was finished, he returned to his law practice.

TO THE WHITE HOUSE

Over the next several years, Lincoln made speeches in support of various candidates but did not seek office. When the Republican Party formed, he soon became a member, for like other Republicans, Lincoln detested slavery. In an 1854 speech, he declared:

> I hate it because of the monstrous injustice of slavery itself. I hate it because it deprives our republican example of its just influence in the world—enables the enemies of free institutions, with plausibility, to taunt us

as hypocrites—causes the real friends of freedom to doubt our sincerity, and especially because it forces so many really good men amongst ourselves into an open war with the very fundamental principles of civil liberty.[8]

Indeed, Lincoln believed that the country's very existence was threatened by slavery. "'A house divided against itself cannot stand,'" he would say, quoting the Bible, "I believe this government cannot endure, permanently, half slave

LINCOLN'S NOMINATION

Journalist Murat Halstead left this newspaper report, excerpted in The Blue and the Gray, *edited by Henry Steele Commager, of Lincoln's victory over William Seward for the Republican Party's presidential nomination in 1860:*

"After adjournment on the second day [May 17] . . . there were few men . . . who believed it possible to prevent the nomination of Seward. His friends . . . had been victorious on every preliminary skirmish. . . . They rejoiced exceedingly, and full of confidence, cried in triumphant tones, "Call the roll of states." . . .

But there was much done after midnight and before the convention assembled on Friday morning [May 18]. There were hundreds . . . who never closed their eyes that night. I saw Henry S. Lane [a Lincoln supporter] . . . , walking from one . . . room to another. . . . He had been toiling with desperation to bring the Indiana delegation to go as a unit for Lincoln. And then in connection with others, he had been operating to bring the Vermonters and the Virginians to the point of deserting Seward.

The Seward men generally abounded in confidence Friday morning. The air was full of rumors of the caucusing [campaigning] the night before, but the opposition . . . was an old story. . . . The Sewardites marched . . . from their headquarters at the Richmond House after their magnificent band, which was brilliantly uniformed. . . .

The most significant vote was that of Virginia, which had been expected solid for Seward, and which now gave him but eight [votes] and gave Lincoln fourteen. Then Indiana gave her twenty-six votes to Lincoln. . . . [On the third ballot with] the change of four votes . . . to Lincoln, . . . the deed was done. . . . There were thousands cheering with the energy of insanity."

LEAVING THE UNION

On December 20, 1860, South Carolina issued the following declaration of secession, reprinted in Fifty Basic Civil War Documents, *edited by Henry Steele Commager:*

"The State of South Carolina having resumed her separate and equal place among nations, deems . . . that she should declare the immediate causes which have led to this act. . . .

In 1787, Deputies were appointed by the States to [draw up] . . . the Constitution of the United States. . . . Thus was established by compact [agreement] between the States, a Government with defined objects and powers, limited to the express words of the grant. . . . We maintain that in every compact between two or more parties, the obligation is mutual; that the failure of one of the contracting parties to perform a material part of the agreement, entirely releases the obligation of the other. . . . The constitutional compact has been deliberately broken and disregarded by the non-slaveholding States; and the consequence follows that South Carolina is released from her obligation. . . . Those [non-slaveholding] States have assumed the right of deciding upon the propriety of our [slaveholding states'] domestic institutions; and have denied the rights of property in . . . the States and recognized by the Constitution; they have denounced as sinful the institution of Slavery; they have permitted the open establishment among them of societies, whose avowed object is to disturb the peace of . . . the citizens of other States. They have encouraged and assisted thousands of our slaves to leave their homes; and those who remain, have been incited by emissaries, books, and pictures, to . . . insurrection."

and half free."[9] Despite these feelings, Lincoln believed that legally nothing could be done about slavery within the Southern states since their rights as states were guaranteed by the Constitution. However, he was equally convinced that slavery could legitimately be kept out of the new western territories. If slavery could not be eliminated, it could be contained, and eventually it might wither away.

In 1858, in part galvanized by the Dred Scott decision, Lincoln sought the Senate seat of Democrat Stephen Douglas. Lincoln failed in his attempt, but a series of debates with Douglas brought him to national attention. Newspapers all over the country reported on the debates and noted how well Lincoln did in these contests. Lincoln used his new fame to win the Republican nomination in 1860 and then the presidency.

SECESSION

The South saw Lincoln's election as a threat to Southern society, which Southerners believed depended on slavery for its very survival. Thus, on December 20, 1860, South Carolina seceded. To justify secession, South Carolinians argued that the U.S. Constitution was a contract between equal partners, the various states, and that any state could withdraw from that agreement at any time if it felt the other parties had violated that compact. South Carolina claimed that the ongoing attempt by Northern abolitionists to end slavery violated the contract between the states. Over the next month and a half, six other Southern states—Alabama, Florida, Georgia, Louisiana, Mississippi, and Texas—would leave the Union.

By no means did all Southerners favor secession. Indeed, many shared the sentiments of Georgian Alexander Stephens:

> In my judgment, the election of no man, constitutionally chosen to that high office [the presidency], is sufficient cause for any State to separate from the Union. It ought to stand by and aid still . . . the Constitution of the country. To make a point of resistance to the Government . . . puts us in the wrong . . . whatever fate is to

befall this country let it never be laid to the charge of the people of the South . . . that we were untrue to our national engagement.[10]

Despite these sentiments, Stephens signed the secession document for his home state of Georgia. Loyalty to state outweighed loyalty to country for many Southerners.

JEFFERSON DAVIS

In February 1861, delegates from the seceding states met in Montgomery, Alabama, and drew up a provisional constitution for the Confederate States of America. Except for the recognition of slavery and acceptance of the rights of slave owners, the document was mostly taken from the U.S. Constitution. According to historian William C. Davis, "It was probably with no sense of irony at all that immediately after the slave provisions, they appended [attached] the old Bill of Rights."[11]

The delegates also elected a provisional president, Jefferson Davis, and vice president, Alexander Stephens. Like Stephens, Davis had initially opposed secession until his home state of Mississippi seceded. The two men were confirmed in their positions by Confederate voters in the first general election in November 1861.

Like his Northern counterpart, Davis was born in Kentucky, although in 1808. Unlike Lincoln, Davis had considerable military and national political experience. He had graduated from the U.S. Military Academy at West Point in 1828 and served in the U.S. Army until 1835, when

LINCOLN SPEAKS

In Lincoln's first inaugural address, found in Fifty Basic Civil War Documents, *edited by Henry Steele Commager, the new president explained his position on slavery and secession.*

"Apprehension seems to exist among the people of the Southern States that . . . a Republican administration [threatens] their property and their peace. . . . I have no purpose, directly or indirectly, to interfere with the institution of slavery in the States where it exists. I believe I have no lawful right to do so, and I have no inclination to do so. . . .

If the United States be not a government proper, but an association of states in the nature of a contract merely, can it as a contract be peacefully unmade by less than all the parties who made it? One party to a contract may violate it—break it, so to speak; but does it not require all to lawfully rescind it? . . .

It follows . . . that no State upon its own . . . can lawfully get out of the Union; that resolves and ordinances to that effect are legally void; and that acts of violence, within any state or states, against the authority of the United States, are insurrectionary. . . .

I therefore consider that . . . the Union is unbroken; and to the extent of my ability I shall take care . . . that the laws of the Union be faithfully executed. . . . I trust that this will not be regarded as a menace, but only as the declared purpose of the Union that it will constitutionally defend and maintain itself."

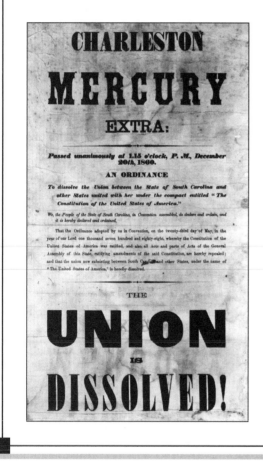

The front page of the Charleston Mercury *announces South Carolina's secession from the Union.*

he resigned to become a plantation owner in Mississippi. In 1848, he led a Mississippi unit in the Mexican War, where he served with distinction and was wounded. Davis had served in both the U.S. House of Representatives and the Senate and, from 1853 to 1857, as secretary of war under President Franklin Pierce.

Jefferson Davis took office as provisional president on February 10, 1861. Abraham Lincoln took office three weeks later on March 4. The stage was now set for the coming conflict.

2 1861: Opening Shots

Less than six weeks after Lincoln's inauguration, war broke out. On April 12, 1861, Confederate forces fired on Union-held Fort Sumter in the harbor of Charleston, South Carolina. Both sides immediately began to build up their armies. Neither side grasped how long the struggle would take or how much it would cost. Indeed, throughout the early months of the war, both North and South were confident of a quick, relatively bloodless conflict.

REACTION TO SECESSION

The reaction among Northerners to secession varied. Some felt that the Southern states should be allowed to leave in peace. Others thought that they should be forced back into the Union.

Lincoln, who did not recognize the right of any state to secede, was determined to reunite the country, no matter the cost. He made it clear, particularly in his inaugural address, that he was even willing to tolerate slavery if such tolerance would keep the nation whole. He made it equally clear that he was prepared to go to war if that were needed. Lincoln was not alone in these feelings.

Historian Bruce Catton observes that "on most points affecting slavery, moderate Republican leaders like Lincoln were prepared to make some adjustments, but they would make no adjustments whatever on the matter of union. . . . They would show a firmness that had not been anticipated."[12]

FORT SUMTER

If Lincoln was prepared to fight to save the Union, the Confederate states were just as determined to fight for their independence. Indeed, they already saw themselves as separate from the United States. The seceding states did not merely leave the Union, they also confiscated federal property: arsenals, military posts, weapons, and harbor facilities, among others, which they saw as now belonging to the Confederacy. Although most of this property was in Confederate hands by Lincoln's inauguration, South Carolina's Fort Sumter was not.

Part of a complex of four forts built to protect Charleston against sea attack, Sumter housed two United States artillery companies under the command of Major Robert Anderson. Despite being a proslavery Kentucky native, Anderson remained loyal to the Union. He refused to surrender Sumter, despite being surrounded by Confederate artillery on the shore and at the other three forts.

By early April, Sumter had been under siege and cut off from supplies for three months. In January, an attempt to resupply the besieged fortress had failed when a Union ship was turned back by cannon fire from the shore. On April 9, with the fort almost out of food, the Lincoln administration dispatched a naval squadron from New York with supplies and reinforcements. Just as the relief expedition reached the mouth of Charleston harbor, the Confederate commander, General Pierre G.T. Beauregard, aware of the fleet's presence, opened fire on Sumter at 4:30 A.M. on April 12.

Seventy guns bombarded Sumter for the next thirty-four hours and did massive damage to the structure. The Union soldiers were too few to fire more than a few of their forty-eight cannons, and

GETTING READY

By the winter of 1861, people, both North and South, began readying for war. This description of Confederate preparations was left by Georgian Mary A. Ward and is found in The Blue and the Gray, *edited by Henry Steele Commager:*

"We began preparing our soldiers for the war. The ladies were all summoned to public places. . . . The sewing-machines were sent to these places and ladies that were known to be experts in cutting out garments were engaged in that part of the work, and every lady in town was turned into a seamstress [to produce uniforms]. . . .

We really did not think that there was going to be an actual war. We had an idea that when our soldiers got upon the ground and showed, unmistakably, that they were really ready and willing to fight—an idea that then, by some sort of hocus pocus, we didn't know what, the whole trouble would be declared at an end. . . . That the feeling existed was beyond doubt from the great disappointment that showed itself afterwards when things turned out differently. . . .

Every soldier, nearly, had a servant with him, and a whole lot of spoons and forks, so as to live comfortably and elegantly in camp, and finally to make a splurge in Washington when they should arrive there, which they expected would be very soon indeed. That is really the way they went off; and their sweethearts gave them embroidered slippers."

Opening Volley Against Sumter

South Carolinian Mary Chesnut witnessed the firing on Fort Sumter and left this description of the opening shots in her diary, A Diary from Dixie:

"April 12th.—Anderson [Sumter's commander] will not capitulate [surrender]. . . . Our peace negotiator . . . came in—that is Mr. Chesnut [Mary's husband] returned. . . . He felt for Anderson and had telegraphed to President Davis for instructions—what answer to give Anderson, etc. . . . He has now gone back to Fort Sumter with additional instructions. . . .

If Anderson does not accept terms at four [a.m.], the orders are, he shall be fired upon. I count four, St. Michael's bells chime out and I begin to hope. At half past four [comes] the heavy booming of a cannon. I sprang out of bed, and on my knees . . . I prayed as I have never prayed before.

There was a sound of stir all over the house, pattering of feet. . . . All seemed hurrying one way. I . . . went, too. It was to the housetop [roof]. The shells were bursting. In the dark I heard a man say, "Waste of ammunition." I knew my husband was rowing about in a boat somewhere in that dark bay, and that the shells were roofing it over, bursting toward the fort. . . . Certainly fire had begun. The regular roar of the cannon, there it was. And who could tell what each volley accomplished of death and destruction. . . .

Do you know after all that noise and our tears and prayers, nobody has been hurt; sound and fury signifying nothing—a delusion and a snare."

Confederate troops fire on Fort Sumter in the opening shots of the Civil War.

their return fire had little effect on their attackers. On the afternoon of April 13, Anderson surrendered. He and his men were allowed to leave the fort the next day. Despite the massive shelling and damage, all of Sumter's defenders survived the attack. During the evacuation, however, two men were killed and four others injured when some ammunition accidentally exploded.

A NEW CRISIS

With the shelling of Fort Sumter, war fever swept both the North and the South. Northerners demanded that the seceding states be forcefully brought back under federal control, and Southerners saw this as the long-awaited first shot in their war of independence.

Both sides were faced with the need to raise large armies. At the time of the firing on Fort Sumter, the U.S. Army had less than seventeen thousand officers and men; they were stationed at posts scattered across the United States and its territories. Additionally, the army's ranks, particularly among the officers, had been reduced by the resignation of many Southerners. The recently formed Confederate army did not number much more. As a result, the bulk of the two armies would be made up of volunteers and draftees.

Lincoln called upon each state to send enough soldiers to make up an army of seventy-five thousand. The nonslave states filled their quotas immediately with volunteers. However, Lincoln's request sparked a crisis with the remaining eight slave states, which had so far remained in the Union: Arkansas, Delaware, Kentucky, Maryland, Missouri, North Carolina, Tennessee, and Virginia. They defied the order. Governor John Letcher of Virginia wrote on April 16:

> I have only to say that the militia of Virginia will not be furnished to the powers at Washington for any such use or purpose as they have in view. Your object is to subjugate the Southern States . . . [,] an object, in my judgment not within the purview [scope] of the Constitution. . . . You have chosen to inaugurate [begin] civil war, and having done so, we will meet it in a spirit as determined as the Administration has exhibited toward the South.[13]

The following day, April 17, Virginia seceded. In May the Confederate Congress, with Jefferson Davis's support, voted to move the Southern capital from Montgomery to Richmond, Virginia. Despite the new capital being perilously close to Union territory—only 100 miles from Washington—Richmond was an important transportation and manufacturing center in the South. It also was in the home state of George Washington and Thomas Jefferson, whose vision had shaped one nation, just as the Confederate leaders hoped theirs would mold another.

BORDER STATES

The other slave states responded much as had Virginia. Arkansas, North Carolina, and Tennessee also seceded, the first two in May and the third in June. The other

WITHIN FORT SUMTER

In the following account, found in The Civil War Archive, *edited by Henry Steele Commager, Union captain Abner Doubleday told what it was like for the defenders of Fort Sumter:*

"[On April 12] showers of [cannon] balls . . . and shells from . . . mortars poured into the fort . . . , causing great flakes of masonry [bricks and stonework] to fall in all directions. When the immense mortar shells, after sailing high in the air, came down in a vertical direction and buried themselves in the parade ground, their explosion shook the fort like an earthquake. . . .

Their missiles were exceedingly destructive to the upper exposed portion of the work [fort], but no essential injury was done to the lower . . . [section] which sheltered us. . . .

About 8 A.M. [on April 13] the officers' quarters were ignited by . . . incendiary shells. . . . The fire was put out, but . . . hot shot [heated metal fired from cannons] soon followed each other so rapidly that it was impossible for us to contend with them any longer. It became evident that the magazine, containing three hundred barrels of powder, would be endangered. . . . While the officers exerted themselves with axes to tear down and cut away all the woodwork in the vicinity, the soldiers were rolling barrels of powder . . . to more sheltered spots. . . .

By 11 A.M. the conflagration [fire] was terrible and disastrous. One fifth of the fort was on fire, and the wind drove the smoke in dense masses into the angle where we had all taken refuge. . . . Had not a slight change of wind taken place, the result might have been fatal to most of us."

Fort Sumter lies in ruins after bombardment from Southern cannons.

Union slave states, now called border states, remained, although the populations of Maryland, Missouri, and Kentucky were sharply divided on the issue of secession and support of the Union or Confederacy. Indeed, Missouri fought its own internal civil war that paralleled the greater national conflict. Delaware, where slavery was on the wane, never seriously considered secession, but all four states did provide soldiers to fight in both armies.

In addition to these four states, there was another border region. In the Virginian secession convention, the western counties voted overwhelmingly against leaving the Union and when Virginia seceded, the western portion broke away. Those counties, which became the state of West Virginia in 1863, had little slavery; their economic ties were more with Ohio and Pennsylvania than with Virginia.

THE NORTHERN STRATEGY

The Union's military strategy had three major goals. In the East, the federal army's goal was to capture Richmond. In the West, it determined to take control of the Mississippi River, thus isolating the western Confederate states from the eastern. And, at sea, the federal navy was to blockade the Confederacy, so as to keep ships from reaching Southern ports with war supplies and other goods that the South's few factories could only make in limited quantities. The blockade was also to keep the South from raising money by selling its cotton and other crops overseas.

The capture of the Mississippi and the blockade were the brainchild of General Winfield Scott, a Virginian, hero of the War of 1812, commander of the U.S.

Army during the Mexican War, and now general in chief. Called the Anaconda Plan because it sought to squeeze the South into submission, Scott's proposal seemed impossible to accomplish because the navy had far too few ships to blockade the immense Southern coastline.

THE SOUTHERN STRATEGY

The Confederacy, on the other hand, decided to fight a more defensive war. The South's goal was to wear down the North until the latter gave up on the conflict and abandoned its desire to force the Southern states back into the Union.

A defensive strategy made good sense for the Confederacy. First, the smaller Southern population could not field an army as large as that of the Union. Second, Confederate soldiers would be defending their homes, a factor that would fuel their determination to win. Third, to take the war into the Union would have meant long supply and communication lines, which would have been difficult to protect from federal attack.

The South had a good model for this plan. George Washington had successfully used a defensive strategy during the Revolutionary War. He rarely attacked unless he held an overwhelming advantage. Washington constantly retreated, even if it meant giving up American territory, to avoid large battles that might destroy his small army. Instead, his soldiers picked off small units of British troops so that the English suffered a constant loss of men and supplies, while the American army stayed relatively constant. Eventually the war simply cost the British too much for them to continue it.

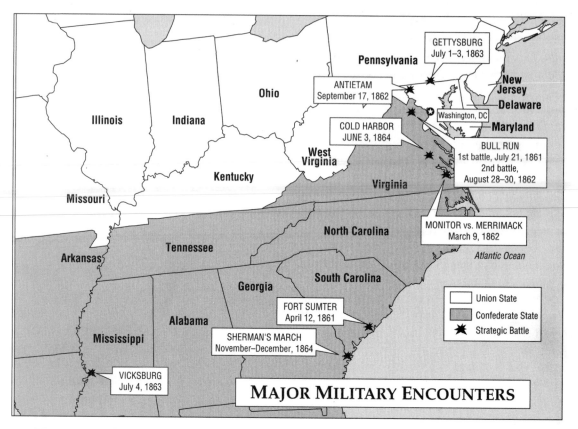

MAJOR MILITARY ENCOUNTERS

GETTYSBURG
July 1–3, 1863

ANTIETAM
September 17, 1862

COLD HARBOR
JUNE 3, 1864

BULL RUN
1st battle, July 21, 1861
2nd battle,
August 28–30, 1862

MONITOR vs. MERRIMACK
March 9, 1862

FORT SUMTER
April 12, 1861

SHERMAN'S MARCH
November–December, 1864

VICKSBURG
July 4, 1863

Pennsylvania
Ohio
New Jersey
Delaware
Washington, DC
Maryland
Illinois
Indiana
West Virginia
Kentucky
Virginia
Missouri
North Carolina
Atlantic Ocean
Arkansas
Tennessee
South Carolina
Georgia
Alabama
Mississippi

☐ Union State
▨ Confederate State
✳ Strategic Battle

However, the Confederate people would not support a military policy based solely on defense, nor would they accept retreat as a major part of that policy. Such a strategy seemed too cowardly. As the *Richmond Examiner* wrote, "The idea of waiting for blows, instead of inflicting them, is altogether unsuited to the genius [nature] of our people."[14]

Additionally, Southern leaders wanted to bring the border states and the southwestern territories into the Confederacy (and in the case of West Virginia, keep it there). Military historian Joseph L. Harsh writes that

> The Southern founding fathers envisioned their country stretching north to the Mason-Dixon line and the Ohio River and west to the Colorado River.

. . . During the war's first six months, Confederate armies marched north and west into Kentucky, Missouri, and Arizona to carry the flag to its natural boundaries.[15]

In the end, the South adopted a defensive-offensive strategy. Whenever possible, Southern troops marched out and fought major battles with invading Northern soldiers. Furthermore, if the opportunity presented itself, the Confederates willingly took the war to the Union by attacking the North.

SKIRMISHES

As spring turned to summer, both sides continued to ready themselves for war. According to the scholar Richard Wheeler:

> Neither side was ready for a major confrontation, but small affairs had begun to occur. Federal naval vessels were exchanging fire with batteries on the Virginia side of the Potomac. . . . There were light encounters on land as the belligerents scouted each other.[16]

In early June, Union forces won a victory in the mountains of the breakaway western Virginia counties. A month later, Confederates defeated federal troops in a small battle in Missouri.

McDowell Marches Out

The first major battle of the war occurred on July 21, 1861, when some thirty-seven thousand Union troops, under the command of General Irvin McDowell, marched into Virginia from Washington to attack Manassas Junction, a railroad hub near the Bull Run River. Most of McDowell's men were recently enlisted volunteers, with almost no training and little discipline. However, insistent demands from Northern politicians that the Union army take action against the South pushed the Lincoln administration into ordering McDowell to make an attack, green troops or no.

Facing the Union army was Beauregard of Sumter fame with twenty-one thousand troops, who were no better trained than McDowell's men. However, unknown to McDowell, General Joseph E. Johnston was sending eleven thousand additional soldiers to reinforce Beauregard's command. Thus McDowell, expecting to outnumber his opponent, was about to meet a force of about the same size.

The Battle of Bull Run

The battle began well for the Federals (that is, federal troops), who pushed the Confederates back. A determined defense by General Thomas Jackson's brigade and a cavalry charge led by General J.E.B. Stuart, however, helped slow the Northern advance. Then, in late afternoon, Johnston's reinforcements appeared and joined Beauregard's men in a mass attack that pushed the Union troops back.

Inexperience plagued the Federals, who instead of retreating in an orderly fashion, fled the field in chaos. The fleeing Northern soldiers were protected to some extent by a regular army unit that provided covering fire. Their real defense, however, came from the Confederates being too disorganized to follow them. In the end, almost three thousand Federals were killed or missing, as opposed to two thousand Confederates.

Victors and Heroes

Hailed as a great victory in the South, the Battle of Bull Run confirmed Confederate belief that the rebels would win and win easily. Southerners saw their cause as being defended by a host of heroes, for this first major engagement made reputations.

One hero who proved invaluable was the Virginian James E.B. "Jeb" Stuart, whose timely cavalry charge had helped turn the tide of the battle. Stuart, a West Point graduate, had been a captain in the U.S. Army before the war, fighting Indians on the Great Plains and keeping the peace in Kansas. He would prove to be one of the best cavalry commanders on either side, and he was one of the most colorful characters in the entire war. Thinking of himself as a swashbuckling hero of old, he wore a plumed hat and a cape, and he loved to take on bold adventures, particularly if he made the newspapers.

STONEWALL JACKSON

And then there was Thomas Jackson, who earned the name "Stonewall" at Bull Run when Confederate general Barnard Bee pointed to Jackson and his men and said, "There is Jackson like a stone wall."[17] His courage under fire and his tactical genius made him one of the outstanding battlefield commanders of the war and brought him admiration from both South and North. In the 1880s, Union officer Joseph C. Tidball wrote of Jackson:

His chief characteristics as a military leader were his quick perceptions of

AT BULL RUN

In a letter home, reprinted in The Union Reader, *edited by Richard B. Harwell, Union soldier Allen A. Kingsbury left this description of action at the Battle of Bull Run:*

"When we ascended a hill we could see men in a field about a mile distant—we could see the glittering of their bayonets. . . . We opened fire upon them; you ought to have seen how they scattered and run into the woods. We fired some three or four rounds among them. . . . Our Co. [company] and Co. G were then ordered into the woods. . . . We had got perhaps three rods [50 feet] . . . when a murderous fire was opened upon us by the rebels from a masked battery [unit of artillery]; several of our men were killed or wounded. Three of my comrades fell dead at my side. . . . I saw a battery on a small hill. I saw an officer . . . beside a cannon; I brought my rifle to my shoulder and fired at him. He threw up his arms and fell headlong down the bank. A perfect volley of rifle shot then rained around me; one bullet . . . cut off my cap. . . . Our Capt. then ordered a retreat. . . . The balls fell like hail around us. . . . When I had got out of the woods . . . , a cannon ball struck the ground . . . behind me, and rebounding, hit me in the joint of the knee . . . and knocked me down. I did not know where I was for several minutes. When I got up I could not stand. Two of the N.Y. 69th took me up and carried me to . . . [a] wagon. . . . I was carried to the hospital."

Supply trains and Union troops race down a road in the Battle of Bull Run.

the weak points of the enemy, his ever readiness, the astounding rapidity of his movements, his sudden and unexpected onslaughts, and the persistency with which he followed them up. His ruling maxim [guideline] was that war meant fighting, and fighting meant killing, and right loyally did he live up to it. Naturally taciturn [reserved], and by habit the keeper of his own designs, it was as difficult for his friends to penetrate them, as it was easy for him to deceive the enemy.[18]

An orphan, with little education, Jackson had had to struggle to make it through West Point. During the Mexican War, however, he displayed his battle savvy and earned two promotions. Bored by life in the peacetime army, he resigned to become a professor at the Virginia Military Institute, where he was teaching when the Civil War broke out. He was not a particularly good teacher: He had to memorize his lectures and had to start at the beginning if interrupted. Consequently, his students called him Tom Fool

Jackson. But many of these same students served under him in the Confederate army and came to prize his abilities as a commanding officer.

IN THE NORTH

News of Bull Run shocked everyone in the North: Lincoln, Scott, the average citizen. Still, despite the loss, the Union was far from beaten. As William Davis notes, "most people in the Union did not lose heart. . . . Rather, the defeat gave them a renewed sense of purpose. National pride and honor had to be avenged."[19] A more realistic attitude toward the scope of the war and the difficulty of winning it emerged in the North. Many now realized that the war was not going to be short, nor the victory easy.

With the defeat at Bull Run, McDowell's term as Union commander came to an end. He was immediately replaced by General George McClellan, who would transform the bedraggled Federal troops into a well-trained army and who would affect much of the course of the war in the East through its second year.

3 1862: The Eastern War

The year 1862 was a seesaw of victory and defeat for both North and South, as their armies clashed in Virginia and Maryland. Yet, regardless of who won the battle each day, by year's end, the war was no closer to a finish than at the beginning. And Southern independence was still neither accomplished nor defeated.

SEEKING FOREIGN HELP

One of the major aims of Confederate leadership was to win foreign recognition, thus lending legitimacy to the South's claim to be a separate country, not a portion of a nation in rebellion. More importantly than legitimacy, however, such recognition, Davis and others believed, could bring economic and possibly military aid from other nations. Consequently, in November 1861, the Confederate government sent representatives to both Great Britain and France.

The South also tried economic blackmail to win foreign aid from Great Britain, whose large textile industry depended upon Southern cotton. Confederate leaders refused to sell the 1861 cotton crop until they received at least some foreign aid from Britain. Davis and others were convinced that, to gain the needed

cotton, English textile manufacturers would pressure their government to recognize and aid the Confederacy. However, this diplomatic policy failed because beginning in 1857 the cotton crops had been so large that England had a huge surplus of raw cotton. Furthermore, the British resented this cotton blackmail and had no intention of giving in to it.

Additionally, by the time the surplus was used up, the Union blockade made any large-scale shipping of Southern cotton impossible. The blockade that had seemed so feeble at its beginning had been strengthened by the purchase of civilian vessels and the building of new warships. By the spring of 1862, the Federal navy had either captured or closed down most of the Confederacy's Atlantic ports, the major exceptions being Charleston and Wilmington, North Carolina. And only swift, small ships, known as blockade runners, could enter even these ports. And blockade runners could carry very little cargo.

BATTLE OF THE IRONCLADS

The Federal navy was not merely blocking trade into and out of Confederate ports; its ships were providing transport

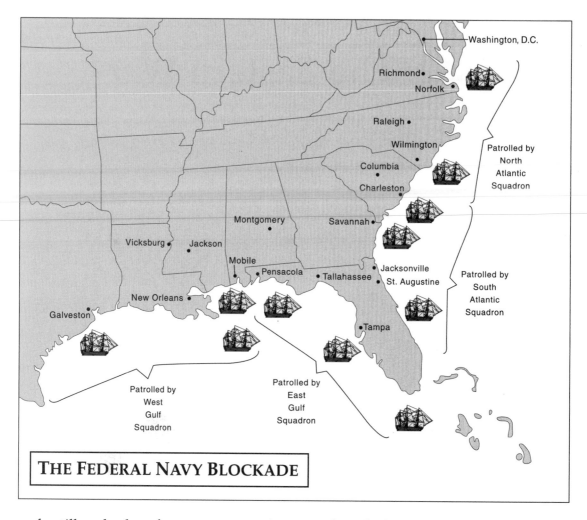

THE FEDERAL NAVY BLOCKADE

and artillery backup for army troops. A combined navy and army operation had secured Roanoke Island, North Carolina, on February 8, 1862, and a month later, on March 14, a Union army commanded by General Ambrose E. Burnside occupied New Bern on the North Carolina mainland.

Thus the Confederate navy needed warships that could destroy the threatening Union vessels. Their answer was the ironclad. At the old Union Norfolk naval station in Virginia, the Confederate navy salvaged the steampowered U.S.S. *Merri-*

mack, which retreating Federals had burned to the waterline the previous year rather than have it fall into enemy hands. As with all naval vessels of the period, the *Merrimack* was made of wood. Southern naval engineers replaced the destroyed upper portion with an enclosed wooden shell, pierced by cannon ports, and covered the entire exposed surface of the craft with iron plate. They renamed the vessel the *Virginia*.

On March 8, 1862, the *Virginia* sailed from Norfolk and destroyed two Union warships in the nearby waters. The ironclad suffered little damage in the fire-fight; cannon shot simply bounced off her metal-covered sides. For the crew inside, however, the noise was often deafening.

The next day, the Confederate ship made to attack a third Federal vessel, but was intercepted by a Union ironclad. Built like a flat raft, it had a swivel gun turret mounted on the deck. This was the *Monitor*, designed by John Ericsson, a famed naval engineer.

The two ironclads battled each other for four hours, with neither ship receiving any serious damage. Finally, the *Monitor* broke away when its captain was wounded by a flying wooden fragment knocked loose by the continual pounding of the *Virginia*'s guns. Although the contest was a draw, it demonstrated the effectiveness of ironclad ships. Both North and South would use them throughout the course of the war.

GEORGE MCCLELLAN

Meanwhile, Union general George McClellan was preparing a major invasion of Virginia to capture Richmond. The thirty-five-year-old major general had graduated second in his class at West Point in 1846 and served with distinction in the Mexican War. Resigning his commission in 1857, he had become the chief engineer

Union general George McClellan surveys the field after a battle.

and vice president for the Illinois Central Railroad. Returning to the army at the outbreak of the war, he had eventually been assigned to the West Virginia campaign, where a series of small victories brought him enough fame for him to be named McDowell's replacement.

An excellent organizer, beginning in August 1861, McClellan rebuilt the defeated army of Bull Run into a new well-trained and disciplined force that he called the Army of the Potomac. Of him, Catton writes:

> McClellan had almost all the gifts. He was young, sturdy, intelligent, and up to a certain point he was very lucky. . . . He won . . . the adoration and the lasting affection of some very tough fighting men who tended to be more cynical about their generals. . . . For a time he served his country most ably.

McClellan, whom his men called "Little Mac," earned the respect of his soldiers by treating them well and seeing that they were well supplied with food and equipment. He often praised their skill and courage, as when he told his West Virginia command that "Soldiers! . . . I fear one thing—that you will not find foeman worthy of your steel."[20]

However, McClellan's relations with his military and civilian superiors were sometimes rocky, particularly with the aging Scott. Eventually, the young general engineered Scott's retirement and became his replacement as commander in chief of the army. McClellan's interaction with Lincoln was not much better; the general barely tolerated the commands and requests for information from the president. Indeed, on one occasion, Mc-

Clellan flatly refused to see Lincoln. The general's combination of administrative skills and arrogance earned him the name "the Young Napoleon," a reference to the early nineteenth-century French ruler who conquered much of Europe.

THE PENINSULA CAMPAIGN

Lincoln had hoped that McClellan would be able to launch a Virginia offensive in late 1861, but the general delayed, claiming that he needed more troops and more time to train his men. His demands for additional troops and more time stretched on for six months. Finally, by early April, McClellan was ready to move. Instead of marching south from Washington into Virginia, he shipped his troops to the tip of a peninsula flanked by the James and York rivers. From there, he planned to move his 105,000-strong army straight up the peninsula to Richmond.

On April 5, only a day after McClellan began his advance, he halted at Yorktown. Convinced on the basis of poor intelligence work that the Confederate defenders outnumbered his command, McClellan set up a siege, which lasted a month while he waited for reinforcements to arrive. In actuality, the Army of the Potomac faced only ten thousand Confederates, whom McClellan's vastly superior numbers could easily have overrun without further troop additions.

DAVIS AND HIS FEUDS

Commanding the Confederate troops that stood between McClellan and Rich-

FINDING FOOD

"The men had not a mouthful to eat, and squads from the different companies obtained permission to forage. . . . I was on one of these details. Leaving the road and striking across the fields, we entered into a yard in the center of which stood a fine brick mansion. We knocked at the door; there was no response. . . . The inmates had fled. . . .

Not an article had been carried off. . . . We entered the dining room; there rested the cat on the window sill; . . . it was difficult to realize that the hostess would not enter and welcome us in a few moments. . . .

Finding nothing in the pantry nor in the kitchen, we went to the spring and filled our canteens with water, then to the dairy at the foot of the hill, and discovered several buckets and cans of milk. . . .

Noticing the loft, a room over the dairy, we climbed up and found it a perfect storeroom. Several barrels were on stands. . . . One of the party . . . showed us a barrel of apple brandy. . . . In the room were a half dozen tubs of apple butter, which we confiscated for the use of our comrades."

mond was General Joseph Johnston, who had an uneasy relationship with Jefferson Davis. The two had recently clashed over which of the five full Confederate generals, one of whom was Johnston, was the senior officer of the entire army. Johnston, believing that his former ranking in the Federal army made him senior, was outraged to find he was ranked fourth. He wrote an angry letter to Davis, who was angered in turn. The two men went on to feud throughout the war.

Indeed, Davis was not an easy man with whom to work. Because of his own military background, he had definite ideas about how the war should be conducted and the army run. For this reason, the Confederate president went through six secretaries of war and quarreled with several of his top generals.

Yet, Davis was almost blindly loyal to those he considered trustworthy and dependable. He kept in command generals, such as Braxton Bragg, who lost far more battles than they won and whose very battlefield ineptness endangered the Confederacy. Historian William C. Davis writes that "Davis did . . . practice favoritism, though he could never see it."[21]

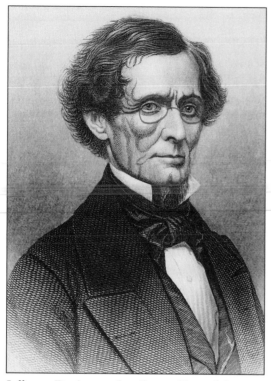

Jefferson Davis served as the president of the Confederacy.

ON TO RICHMOND

While McClellan besieged Yorktown, Confederate reinforcements converged on Richmond. By early May, Johnston had some sixty-five thousand troops, although McClellan overestimated those numbers. When on May 5, the Federals finally attacked Yorktown, they found the Confederates had abandoned the city and pulled back to Richmond.

McClellan pushed down the peninsula until his advance units could actually see church spires in the Confederate capital. Facing them were trenches filled with Southern defenders. McClellan prepared for another siege and demanded further reinforcements.

JACKSON'S VALLEY CAMPAIGN

Meanwhile, Union forces were busy fighting Stonewall Jackson in the Shenandoah Valley in western Virginia. The broad, generally flat valley was a major farming region and would prove an excellent highway for armies moving into and out of the state. By March 1862, the Union had an army of thirty-eight thousand under the command of General Nathan Banks in the valley. On March 23, Jackson with only six thousand men attacked Banks at Kernstown and suffered the only loss of his career.

Jackson soon regrouped and added another eleven thousand soldiers to his command. In early May, General John C. Frémont moved in from the west, planning to link his unit with that of Banks. On May 8, to prevent this combining of Union forces, Jackson attacked and smashed Frémont's advance guard at the mountain village of McDowell and then chased the remaining Frémont troops north to the town of Franklin. The Confederate general now turned east and on May 23 hit Banks, whom the Confederates drove back first to Winchester and then across the Potomac River into Maryland. Not being authorized to invade Union territory, Jackson stopped his advance at Harpers Ferry on the Virginia side of the river.

Concerned with the nearness of Jackson to Washington, Lincoln ordered Banks and Frémont, as well as Irvin McDowell, who was at Fredericksburg, Virginia, to converge quickly on Harpers Ferry. Lincoln hoped this would trap Jackson in the town. However, Jackson learned from scouts of the Federal maneuver and abandoned Harpers Ferry on May 31. In a quick march he eluded the trap, some of his troops only making it into the clear by a few hours after having marched fifty miles in two days.

Frémont and McDowell, however, were in hot pursuit, so Jackson wheeled his troops quickly. He first defeated Frémont at Cross Keys on June 8 and McDowell at Port Republic the next day. The Federals then retreated.

Jackson's exploits made him the most famous battlefield commander of the war. In a single month, he had won several battles against a numerically superior enemy, thus gaining control of the Shenandoah. Because infantry traditionally moved slowly, as compared with the much faster and more mobile mounted cavalry, Jackson's swiftly maneuvering foot soldiers earned the name "foot cavalry."

SEVEN PINES

Jackson's valley campaign also temporarily diverted Union troops that had been slated to join McClellan at Richmond. On May 31, Johnston decided to strike before Federal reinforcements could be released from the now finished Shenandoah campaign. He launched an attack on McClellan's line at the town of Seven Pines. The attack was poorly executed and was repulsed.

The failure at Seven Pines cost the Confederates dearly. They lost almost 10 percent of their fighters. Among the casualties was a badly wounded Joseph Johnston. On June 1, Jefferson Davis named as Johnston's replacement his next senior general, Robert E. Lee.

Confederate general Robert E. Lee (left) meets with his chief lieutenant, Stonewall Jackson.

ROBERT E. LEE

Lee, the son of Revolutionary War hero "Light Horse" Harry Lee, was born in Virginia in 1807. Graduating second in his class from West Point in 1829, he served in both the U.S. Army engineers and cavalry. He saw action in the 1848 Mexican War, was superintendent of West Point from 1852 to 1855, and led the troops that ended John Brown's raid on Harpers Ferry.

On April 18, 1861, the day following Virginia's secession, Colonel Lee turned down an offer to command all U.S. Army forces, resigning instead because he could not fight against his home state. Returning to Virginia, he became a general in the Confederate army and was soon assigned to West Virginia, which he failed to reconquer. In early 1862, he became Jefferson Davis's military advisor, the role in which he was serving when Johnston was wounded. Up to this point Lee's war record was undistinguished, and he did not impress his new command. One wrote that "he is a large, stout man, somewhat inclined to corpulence [fat], . . . [who] makes no show . . . and rides . . . as quietly as a farmer."[22]

One of Lee's first acts was to rename the force under him the Army of Northern Virginia. His two chief lieutenants were Jackson, pulled back from the valley for the defense of Richmond, and General James Longstreet. The cavalry detachment was headed by Jeb Stuart.

On June 25, Lee's new command attacked the Army of the Potomac. Over the next week, a period of time that earned the battle the name Seven Days', the Confederates hit hard at Union lines. Again, McClellan overestimated the num-

bers of his foes and fell back. By July 1, he was back at the tip of the peninsula, not far from where he had begun his drive toward Richmond three months before. Safe under the guns of naval warships, the Northern general settled down and offered no new offensives.

SECOND BULL RUN

During the Seven Days' Battle, both sides suffered heavy losses: fifteen thousand for the Federals and twenty thousand for the Confederates. The smaller Southern army could ill afford to lose so many men, and mounting casualties were a constant worry for Lee. Still, McClellan was no longer an immediate threat to Richmond.

Meanwhile, Lincoln realized that the Peninsula campaign had failed. In despair over his overcautious general, he appointed General John Pope to combine the men under Banks, Frémont, and McDowell in an attack on Richmond. Pope, a successful campaigner against the Confederacy along the Mississippi, lost the respect of his new command when he told them that his western soldiers were superior fighters. Pope also appeared foolish when he reportedly said that his headquarters would be in the saddle. Robertson notes, "Confederate wags had a field day deriding a big-mouthed enemy general who put his headquarters where his hindquarters ought to be."[23]

In mid-July, Pope left Washington and crossed the Potomac into Virginia. To oppose him, Lee sent Jackson, who stopped the Union advance at the Battle of Cedar Mountain on August 9. Lincoln then ordered the Army of the Potomac to withdraw from the peninsula so that it could be sent to reinforce Pope. With the withdrawal of McClellan and the end of any immediate threat to Richmond, Lee was free to move the remainder of his troops west to link up with Jackson.

On August 28, with McClellan and Lee still in transit, Pope and Jackson met in the Second Battle of Bull Run. For the next two days, Pope sent out his units one at a time; the Southerners easily beat back these attacks. Then, on August 30, unknown to Pope, Lee and thirty thousand troops reached the battle site. While Pope was making another of his assaults against Jackson's position, Lee sent Longstreet in a mass attack. Taken completely by surprise, the Northern line collapsed. The Federals retreated and, for two days, were harassed by the Confederates before the Union troops escaped across the Potomac.

INTO MARYLAND

Taking advantage of the second Bull Run victory and with Davis's permission, on September 4, Lee took the Army of Northern Virginia into Maryland. The arguments against such an invasion were many. Lee wrote Davis:

> The army is not properly equipped for an invasion of an enemy's territory. It lacks much of the material of war, is feeble in transportation, the animals being much reduced, and the men are poorly provided with clothes, and in thousands of instances, are destitute of shoes. . . . What occasions me the most concern is the fear of getting out of ammunition.[24]

Despite Lee's misgivings, there were several compelling reasons for invading Maryland. Both Lee and Davis hoped that slave-state Maryland would feed the invading Confederates and add new soldiers to their ranks (many thousands of Marylanders already marched in the Army of Northern Virginia). A further consideration was the possibility that a victory on Northern soil, coming on the heels of two months of successful campaigning, might win the Confederacy the foreign recognition it sought. Finally, Lee had no desire to give up the momentum of his string of victories and return passively to Richmond.

ORDER 191

Once more facing Lee was McClellan and the Army of the Potomac, swelled with the addition of Pope's men. (The disgraced Pope had been shipped off to Minnesota to fight the Native American Sioux, and McDowell, who had had the misfortune to be at both battles at Bull Run, was exiled to California.) Counting on McClellan's now well-known slowness, Lee split his command in two, sending Jackson back to Harpers Ferry to capture the Federal garrison there, while he rode into Maryland. McClellan learned about this maneuver when a Union soldier found a copy of Lee's order 191 wrapped around three cigars. Instead of immediately marching out to crush Lee's much-reduced force, however, McClellan delayed sixteen hours. By the time he did move out on September 14, his advantage was lost. A spy had warned Lee of the lost order.

Heavily outnumbered, Lee began to withdraw back to Virginia, but on

September 15, he heard that Jackson had captured Harpers Ferry and was coming to rejoin the main Southern army. Lee now felt he had the numbers to battle McClellan and halted his troops near Sharpsburg, Maryland, along Antietam Creek. On September 16, Jackson and most of his unit arrived. The remaining five thousand of Jackson's troops, under the command of General Ambrose P. Hill, had temporarily remained behind to handle the surrender of twelve thousand Federal soldiers.

ANTIETAM

On September 17, McClellan and his army of seventy-five thousand attacked Lee's thirty-eight thousand troops. Cautious as ever, the Northern general sent only a portion of his force to fight Lee at any one time. Still, the repeated Federal attacks finally shattered the Confederate main defense line, which was in a sunken road that came to be known as Bloody Lane. Yet again, McClellan's caution held him in check. Instead of advancing farther, he was content to hold the captured road.

Fighting now concentrated three miles south of Bloody Lane. Here, Union troops, under General Ambrose Burnside, faced intense fire as they tried to capture a bridge that would let them cross the Antietam for an assault on Confederate positions. The Federals eventually succeeded in taking the bridge and were pushing Lee's men back when Hill arrived from Harpers Ferry and launched a fierce counterattack that drove off the northerners.

Antietam was the bloodiest single day of the war. A total of twelve thou-

sand Northerners and ten thousand Southerners were killed or wounded. Believing that his army was crippled by its losses, McClellan did not continue fighting the next day. For the same reason, Lee chose not to renew the battle, and that night, the Army of Northern Virginia slipped south, back over the Potomac to Virginia. The Northern commander followed on September 19 but was stopped just across the Potomac by stiff Confederate resistance.

THE EMANCIPATION PROCLAMATION

Antietam was an indecisive battle with no clear winner. However, it did put an end to Lee's northern invasion and sent him into Virginia. Therefore, Lincoln, in need of a Union victory against the Army of Northern Virginia, declared it one. In part, the president needed a victory to bolster sagging Federal morale, but he had also been waiting for a Union win to issue the Emancipation Proclamation, an executive order that freed the slaves of any state still in rebellion on January 1, 1863. Although the proclamation, issued on September 22, did not abolish slavery in the United States, it was the first step in that direction. It also elevated the war to a higher moral plane since the ending of slavery was, along with reuniting the country, now one of the major goals of Union victory.

The Emancipation Proclamation also declared that African Americans could enlist in the Federal army. Anxious to fight, black Americans until now had been able to serve only as laborers. Widespread prejudice made Union soldiers

The Wounding of a General

The Battle of Antietam was one of the bloodiest of the war. In John B. Gordon's 1903 Reminiscences of the Civil War, *excerpted in* The Blue and the Gray, *edited by Henry Steele Commager, Gordon, a Confederate general, wrote of the deadly fight that left him with five wounds:*

"The first volley from the Union lines in my front sent a . . . ball [bullet] through my right leg. . . . Both sides stood in the open at short range . . . and the firing was doing a deadly work. Higher up in the same leg I was again shot. . . . When later in the day the third ball pierced my left arm, tearing asunder the tendons and mangling the flesh, they [his soldiers] caught sight of the blood running down my fingers, and . . . pleaded with me to leave them and go to the rear. . . . I could not consent to leave them, in such a crisis. . . . There was no way of stanching [stopping] the blood, but I had a vigorous constitution, and this was doing me good service.

A fourth ball ripped through my shoulder, leaving its base and a wad of clothing in its track. I could still stand and walk, although the shock and loss of blood had left little of my normal strength. . . .

I was shot down by a fifth ball, which struck me squarely in the face, and passed out, barely missing the jugular vein. I fell forward and lay unconscious with my face in my cap. . . . I was borne on a litter [stretcher] to the rear, and recall nothing more till revived by stimulants at a late hour of the night."

hostile to the idea of black troops. Now, with presidential approval, the first black battle units were immediately formed, although the officers remained white and the African American soldiers were paid less than white troopers.

Reaction to the Proclamation

Issuing such a proclamation was a risky move on Lincoln's part. Even though it did not affect slavery in the border states, it still angered many slaveholders in those areas and might have loosened the Federal government's shaky hold on the region. The proclamation also angered many in the army, who, though willing to fight for their country, were less keen about, if not downright hostile toward the idea of fighting for African American freedom.

Those angered by the proclamation charged that, in issuing it, Lincoln had

A Union medic stands amid tents where he treated both Union and Confederate wounded after the Battle of Antietam.

exceeded his constitutional authority. As McPherson points out, however, "such remarks missed the point. . . . Lincoln acted under his war powers to seize enemy resources."[25] Indeed, many in the army saw the president's act in this light. Others genuinely despised slavery and gladly fought to end it.

Foreign reaction to the proclamation was initially lukewarm but quickly grew enthusiastic, particularly in Great Britain. Long a champion of abolition, Britain had been instrumental in ending the international slave trade early in the century. The U.S. minister to England wrote that "It is quite clear that the current is now setting very strongly with us among the body of the people."[26] To promote recognition of the Confederacy now meant being pro-slavery, a position from which British politicians hurriedly distanced themselves.

FREDERICKSBURG

After Antietam, President Lincoln was convinced that Lee's men were in far worse shape than McClellan's and that this was the moment for McClellan to strike and destroy the Army of Northern Virginia. Thus, on November 7, after six weeks of inactivity on McClellan's part, a disgusted Lincoln named Burnside to replace the man that the press had come to call "Mac the Unready." In historian Richard Wheeler's assessment,

McClellan could have been a first-rate field commander, for along with his . . . knowledge of strategy and tactics, he had the absolute trust of his troops. Unfortunately, he was wholly without a spirit of daring. It was true that while he was preparing an advance on the foe he issued bold pronouncements about his intentions, but as soon as he made contact he began to fear defeat and became paralyzingly cautious.[27]

Burnside, on the other hand, got his 115,000 troops moving south into Virginia without delay. He planned to cross the Rappahannock River, take Fredericksburg, and then march on Richmond. By moving swiftly, his force could arrive

---

THE ARGUMENT FOR AFRICAN AMERICAN SOLDIERS

Although African Americans would eventually serve as Union soldiers, initially they were refused entry into the army. In the following article, reprinted in The Life and Writings of Frederick Douglass, *edited by Philip S. Foner, the abolitionist and former slave Frederick Douglass argued elegantly in favor of African Americans being enlisted in the Union army:*

"What upon earth is the matter with the American government and people? . . . They are sorely pressed . . . by a vast army of slaveholding rebels. . . . Every resource of the nation, whether of men or money, whether of wisdom or strength, could be well employed to avert the impending ruin. . . . The demands of the hour are not comprehended by the Cabinet or the crowd. Our President, Governors, Generals and Secretaries are calling . . . [,] "Men! men! send us men!" . . . or the cause of the Union is gone. . . . ; and yet these very officers . . . persistently refuse to receive the very class of men which have a deeper interest in the defeat . . . of the rebels, than all others. . . .

Why does the Government reject the Negro? Is he not a man? Can he not wield a sword, fire a gun, march and countermarch, and obey orders like any other? Is there the least reason to believe that a regiment of well-drilled Negroes would deport [conduct] themselves less soldier-like on the battle field than the raw troops gathered up generally from the towns and cities. . . ? We do believe that such soldiers, . . . would set the highest example of order and good behavior to their fellow soldiers, and in every way add to the national power."

THE EMANCIPATION PROCLAMATION

After the Army of Northern Virginia was turned back at Antietam, President Lincoln issued the Emancipation Proclamation, excerpted from Fifty Basic Civil War Documents, *edited by Henry Steele Commager:*

"On the first day of January, A.D. 1863, all persons held as slaves within any State or designated part of a State the people whereof shall then be in rebellion against the United States shall be then, thenceforward, and forever free; and the executive government of the United States, including the military and naval authority thereof, will recognize and maintain the freedom of such persons and will do no act or acts to repress such persons . . . in any efforts they may make for their actual freedom.

That the executive will on the first day of January . . . designate the States and parts of States, if any, in which the people . . . shall then be in rebellion against the United States; and the fact that any State or the people thereof shall on that day be in good faith represented in the Congress of the United States by members chosen thereto at elections in which a majority of the qualified voters of such States shall have participated shall . . . be deemed conclusive evidence that such State and the people thereof are not then in rebellion against the United States. . . .

I . . . enjoin upon the people so declared to be free to abstain from all violence. . . . And I further declare . . . that such persons . . . will be received into the armed service of the United States to garrison forts, positions, stations, and other places, and to man vessels of all sorts in said service."

Freed slaves cheer as President Lincoln greets the public after issuing the Emancipation Proclamation.

and overwhelm the small Confederate garrison at Fredericksburg before Lee could reach it with reinforcements.

On November 17, the Army of the Potomac arrived at the Rappahannock, well ahead of the Army of Northern Virginia. However, the pontoon bridges the troops needed to cross the river to Fredericksburg had not. It would be a month before Burnside made the crossing on December 13. By then, Lee had seventy-eight thousand troops stationed on or around the hills overlooking Fredericksburg. In front of the central heights was a stone wall, behind which was a sunken road in which Longstreet's command took shelter. From the top of the hills and from behind the wall, the Confederates laid down a deadly fire, which eventually sent the Army of the Potomac back across the Rappahannock. The Federals had lost thirteen thousand killed or wounded, more than twice the Army of Virginia's losses.

The ease of Lee's victory was greeted with joy throughout the South. In the North, gloom reigned as winter set in. Even word from the western campaign, which had generally been good for the Union for much of 1862, was bad.

4 1862: The Western War

The battle for the Mississippi River and the region between it and the Appalachian Mountains was for the Union almost as important as the struggle to capture Richmond. Although the Confederacy had no desire to lose control of this region, it lacked the human and material resources to mount an effective defense and still counter Federal offensives in Virginia.

THE RIVER WAR

At the beginning of 1862, only 48,000 Confederate troops guarded the border between North and South that stretched from the Appalachians to the Mississippi. The Union, on the other hand, had more than 100,000 soldiers, as well as naval units on the rivers, preparing for invasion. The Mississippi was by no means the only important river in the area. Indeed, for both sides the key to victory in this area was control of the rivers, many of which run north to south, thus forming natural highways into Tennessee, Alabama, and Mississippi. Consequently, just south of the Kentucky border, the Confederacy had placed a single fort each on the Tennessee and Cumberland rivers.

A combined Federal navy-army force set out to capture these forts in early 1862. Commodore Andrew H. Foote was in command of seven gunboats, and General Ulysses S. Grant led fifteen thousand Union soldiers.

ULYSSES S. GRANT

Hiram Ulysses Grant, born in 1822 in Ohio, became Ulysses Simpson Grant through a clerical error when he entered West Point. He detested the military academy and excelled only in horsemanship, graduating twenty-first of thirty-nine in his 1843 class. With grades too poor to qualify for the cavalry, he became an infantry and later quartermaster officer, serving in the Mexican War and then in California. In 1854, with rumors of heavy drinking swirling around him, Grant resigned from the army.

The next few years saw a string of business failures as Grant first tried his hand at farming and then selling both firewood and real estate. In 1861, unable to get an engineering position in St. Louis, he became a clerk in his family's leather goods store in Galena, Illinois.

When war broke out, Grant's offer to return to uniform was ignored by the

War Department and then turned down by George McClellan. As Catton observes, "Grant had been typed: a drifter and a drunkard. . . . Everybody in the Old Army liked . . . Grant, but nobody seemed to have much confidence in him."[28] However, in June 1861 he became a colonel with the Twenty-first Illinois Infantry; by the end of July, he had been promoted to brigadier general. He owed both ranks to his neighbor and friend Illinois congressman Elihu B. Washburne.

Stationed at Cairo, Illinois, Grant conducted operations in Kentucky and Missouri. In September 1861, he prevented Confederate takeovers of Paducah and Smithland, Kentucky. Two months later, at Belmont, Missouri, he found himself

Union general Ulysses S. Grant reads a letter in camp before the siege of Fort Donelson.

and his command surrounded, and when several panic-stricken officers recommended surrender Grant replied, "We had cut our way in and could cut our way out [escape] just as well."[29] Such cool level-headedness under fire would be one of Grant's hallmarks.

FORT HENRY AND FORT DONELSON

Under pressure from Washington to move more forcefully against the rebels, area commander General Henry Halleck ordered Grant and Foote to attack Fort Henry on the Tennessee River. On February 6, the Federals reached their target, which boasted only seventeen cannons and was built on such low ground that it was often flooded. The navy's steam-powered, paddle-wheeled gunboats, four of which had their machinery protected by iron plate and which could make their way through as little as six feet of water, had no trouble pounding the fort into submission. Most of the Southern garrison, however, escaped east to the Confederacy's Fort Donelson on the Cumberland River.

On February 12, Grant and his soldiers reached and surrounded Donelson, now reinforced by fifteen thousand Confederates from Nashville. Late the next day, Foote's task force arrived. Much better armed and situated than Fort Henry, Donelson repulsed a naval attack on February 14, sinking the gunboat *St. Louis* and wounding Foote.

The next day, feeling themselves outnumbered and outgunned, the Confederates decided to abandon the fort and make a break for Nashville. They came close to punching a hole through Grant's lines, but indecision among the Southern officers allowed Grant time to rally his men and push the Southerners back into Donelson. The next morning, February 16, Grant demanded and received the unconditional surrender of the fort, earning him the name of "Unconditional Surrender" Grant. He took thirteen thousand Confederates prisoner. Some twenty-five hundred infantry, as well as the cavalry unit, managed to escape by making their way through a nearby swamp.

ALBERT SIDNEY JOHNSTON

With the fall of Donelson, it took Union troops and gunboats only a week to reach and capture Nashville on February 23. Indeed, the loss of both forts left the entire trans-Appalachian South open to Northern invasion. Grant himself followed the Tennessee River south toward Mississippi.

General Albert Sidney Johnston, in charge of the Confederate West, now withdrew his forces from central Kentucky and Tennessee and relocated his own headquarters from the fallen Nashville to Corinth, Mississippi. Another of the many West Pointers in both armies and a close friend of Jefferson Davis, Johnston had resigned from the army in 1834 and joined the revolt that freed Texas from Mexico. After the Mexican War, in which he commanded a Republic of Texas unit, he rejoined the U.S. Army, rising to the rank of brigadier general before his second resignation in 1861. At the beginning of the war, many in the North and South considered him to be the finest officer on either side, although Grant would later criticize Johnston as indecisive and overly cautious.

SHILOH: FIRST DAY

Grant's assessment notwithstanding, on April 6, Johnston, along with Pierre Beauregard, was able to ambush the Northern commander at Pittsburg Landing, a small Tennessee town just twenty-three miles from Corinth. Johnston's plan was to cut the Federals off from the river and push them into a nearby swamp. Although the Confederates took Grant completely by surprise, they failed in their objective. In part the failure came when hungry rebels overrunning the Northern camp began looting it for food instead of chasing the enemy. But, in large part, the attack failed because of stiff Union resistance around the Shiloh Church, which gave the battle its name, and a dense patch of oak trees, where so many bullets flew that it was called the hornet's nest.

In midafternoon, Johnston was hit in the leg. With an artery cut, he bled to death quickly. Beauregard took command, but as night fell the Federals were still unbeaten and had found safety along the banks of the river.

SHILOH: SECOND DAY

During the night, Union reinforcements arrived, and Grant launched a fierce counterattack the next day. The fresh Northern troops pushed hard against Beauregard's now exhausted soldiers. At the end of the day, the Confederates retreated back to Corinth.

The heavy losses both sides sustained, more than twenty-three thousand casualties total, shocked everyone and foretold the slaughter that battles in the East would produce later in the year and throughout

AT SHILOH

Union soldier Leander Stillwell left the following account of the fierce fighting at Shiloh, excerpted in The Blue and the Gray, *edited by Henry Steele Commager:*

"We began firing at once. From one end of the regiment to the other leaped a sheet of red flame. . . . We had fired . . . two or three rounds when . . . we were ordered to fall back. . . . We halted . . . in front of our tents, and again began firing. . . . Here we did our first hard fighting during the day. Our officers said . . . that we held the line an hour and ten minutes. How long it was I do not know. I 'took no note of time.'

We retreated. . . . I think we did not fall back a minute too soon. As I rose . . . , I saw men in gray . . . clothes, . . . running through the camp on our right. . . . I ran down our company street, and . . . I thought of my knapsack with all my . . . belongings, including that precious little packet of letters from home. I said to my self, 'I will save my knapsack, anyhow,' but one quick backward glance over my left shoulder made me change my mind. . . . I never saw my knapsack or any of its contents afterwards.

Our broken forces halted and reformed. . . . We . . . relieved a regiment . . . [that had been] desperately engaged . . . for four hours. . . . About the first thing that met my gaze . . . [were] dead [Union] men in blue; some doubled up face downward, others with their white faces upturned to the sky. . . . Here we stayed until our last cartridge was shot away. We were then relieved by another regiment."

---

the entire war. Grant was harshly criticized for the heavy Union losses, and cries went up for his removal. Lincoln responded simply, "I can't spare this man. He fights."[30]

However, as a concession to Grant's critics, the president did place Halleck in direct charge of the remainder of the campaign, which ended on May 30 with the capture of Corinth. Beauregard retreated to central Mississippi. By taking Corinth,

through which the only east-west Southern rail line passed, the Union severed one of the major links between the western and eastern Confederacy.

ACTION ON THE UPPER MISSISSIPPI

While Grant and Halleck were fighting in Tennessee and Mississippi, other Union forces were active on the Mississippi

River. On March 3, another army-navy unit, under the command of Pope and Foote, besieged New Madrid, Missouri, and Tennessee's Island Number 10, located near the Kentucky border. The two fortified positions fell on April 8.

The next target was Fort Pillow, Tennessee, which stood between the Union forces and Memphis and which came under heavy naval fire beginning in mid-April. On May 10, the Federal fleet was attacked by the Confederate River Defense Fleet, a collection of miscellaneous boats armored with wood and cotton bales and crewed by the Confederate army. The Confederates managed to ram and sink two Union ironclads before being driven off.

Three weeks later, on June 4, Fort Pillow was evacuated, and the Northern task force sailed downriver to Memphis, arriving two days later. Here, the Defense Fleet once more attacked the Federals, but this time three of the Confederate craft were destroyed and four captured. Memphis surrendered immediately.

FARRAGUT ON THE LOWER MISSISSIPPI

New Orleans, some 100 miles up the Mississippi from the Gulf of Mexico, was the Confederacy's largest and most cosmopolitan city. Until the tightening naval blockade had stopped sea traffic, it was also one of the wealthiest and busiest ports in North America.

The Union wanted very much to capture New Orleans, and in mid-April, a small fleet of oceangoing warships steamed north on the Mississippi to do just that.

The task force was led by Commodore David G. Farragut, who had served in the navy since he was nine and who had seen action in the War of 1812 and along the east coast during the first year of the Civil War. Although a Southerner by birth, he proved himself a loyal, determined, and daring Union commander.

Preventing Farragut's access to New Orleans were two forts, Jackson and St. Philip, which sat on opposite banks of the river. Just beyond them, a chain, fastened to a series of dismasted schooners, stretched across the river. Naval historian Ivan Musicant writes:

> Behind this barrier ranged the Confederate forces afloat, about eighteen vessels, as heterogeneous [mixed] a

David G. Farragut served as commodore in the Union navy.

lot as ever cast an anchor, initially reporting to three separate—and feuding—commands. The gunboats . . . , the ironclad . . ., and some tugs . . . and armed launches were of the regular Confederate Navy. . . . [Two] big steamers, cottonclad rams . . . , owed their allegiance to the Louisiana Provisional Navy. Six other cottonclads belonged to the army River Defense Fleet. General Lovell [in charge of New Orleans] tried to place them under naval command, but that was politically impossible. As he later ruefully noted, the army's rivermen proved "unable to govern themselves, and unwilling to be governed by others."[31]

If the Federal fleet could pass these obstacles, little else defended the city, for most of its garrison had been ordered north to fight in Tennessee.

THE CAPTURE OF NEW ORLEANS

For six days, mortars mounted on some of Farragut's ships pounded the two forts, doing considerable damage but failing to put the Confederate guns out of commission. On the night of April 24, the commodore ordered his ships to sail as swiftly as possible through the gap between Jackson and St. Philips. Several nights before, he had had a party go upriver and sink enough of the schooners and the chain to clear a path along the eastern bank of the river.

It was a harrowing passage, but most of the task force made it. Neither of the forts proved to have sufficient firepower to stop the Union fleet, and the rebel boats

Union general Benjamin F. Butler, known to Southerners as "Beast" Butler, poses in his tent.

were quickly dealt with by the more heavily armed Union warships. When word of the Federals' approach arrived at New Orleans, the remaining Confederate troops left the city in order to save it from bombardment by Farragut.

The city was soon occupied by Union troops commanded by General Benjamin F. Butler, whose harsh rule would earn him the hatred of the citizens of the city and most of the South. Butler hanged one man for tearing down the American flag.

And, after a series of incidents in which women insulted or spit on Federal soldiers and one dumped a chamber pot on Farragut as he walked a New Orleans street, the Union general ordered that such women be treated as prostitutes and thrown in jail. The last act earned him the name "Beast" Butler.

THE LAST CITADEL

By early June, only one Confederate city still stood on the Mississippi River: Vicksburg. Perched atop high bluffs, Vicksburg, Mississippi, is about halfway between Memphis and New Orleans. Catton writes:

> Vicksburg was just waiting for someone to come and capture it. Hasty fortifications had been built, eighteen guns had been mounted, and 3600 infantry had been assembled. . . . Two divisions from [Union area commander] Halleck's army could have taken the place with ease. . . . But Halleck was still digesting Corinth.[32]

Thus, Farragut, now promoted to admiral, was sent with his fleet to try battering the city into submission. However, Vicksburg was too high above the river for the ships' guns to have much effect. Abandoning the effort, Farragut eventually sailed back to New Orleans in early August. By then, the city's Confederate garrison had swollen to ten thousand, and its defenses had grown stronger.

Almost immediately upon Farragut's departure, Confederate troops reoccupied the river between Vicksburg and Port Hudson, Louisiana. Thus, a small corridor was kept open that connected the eastern Confederacy with the far western states.

BEYOND THE MISSISSIPPI

The conflict west of the Mississippi River did not receive the attention by either side that the battles east of it did. Still, warfare over Missouri resulted in much fierce fighting that culminated on March 7 and 8 in the Battle of Pea Ridge, Arkansas. Some twelve thousand Federals held off an attack by twenty thousand Confederates, which included several thousand Native Americans from the Indian Territory (present-day Oklahoma). This victory gave the Union control of southern Missouri and northern Arkansas.

The far west also saw its share of combat when Texas units invaded the New Mexico Territory. Beginning in February, the Texans successfully occupied much of the region, including the cities of Santa Fe and Albuquerque, and even pushed as far west as Tucson in the Arizona Territory. However, Union forces from California soon routed the Arizona Confederates, and a series of Confederate defeats in New Mexico, the most important of which was at Glorieta Pass in March, saw the rebels retreat back to Texas by the end of July.

CONFEDERATE RAIDERS

In early July, Union general Don Carlos Buell, who had reinforced Grant at Shiloh, moved east with forty thousand troops to take Chattanooga, Tennessee. To stop him, two Confederate cavalry leaders, John

Hunt Morgan and Nathan Bedford Forrest, launched raids to disrupt Buell's supply lines. Neither commander had any formal military training, although Morgan had fought in a volunteer unit in the Mexican War, yet both proved to be canny, resourceful, and dangerous opponents.

On July 4, Morgan, formerly a merchant in Lexington, Kentucky, led a band of fellow Kentuckians in a series of raids in his home state. Over the next three weeks, the raiders destroyed railroad tracks, telegraph lines, bridges, and supply depots and captured twelve hundred prisoners. In a second series of raids in August, Morgan and his men collapsed an eight-hundred-foot railroad tunnel that cut Buell off from

AN OVERRATED GENERAL

Before his death at the Battle of Shiloh, Albert Sidney Johnston was ranked among the ablest officers of either side. However, Ulysses S. Grant in his 1885 Personal Memoirs of U.S. Grant *had another take on the Southern general:*

"My judgment . . . is that he [Johnston] was vacillating [wavering] and undecided in his actions.

All the [Confederate] disasters in Kentucky and Tennessee were so discouraging to the authorities in Richmond that Jefferson Davis wrote an unofficial letter . . . expressing his own anxiety. . . . [Johnston] had evidently become so disturbed . . . that he resolved to strike out in an offensive campaign. . . . We have the authority of his son and biographer for saying that his plan was to attack the forces at Shiloh and crush them. . . . The design was a bold one; but we have the same authority for saying that in the execution Johnston showed vacillation and indecision. . . . Beauregard, his second in command, was opposed to the attack. . . . Johnston not only listened to . . . Beauregard . . . , but held a council of war on the subject. . . . On the evening of the same day he was in consultation with some of his generals on the same subject, and still again on the [next] morning. During this last consultation and before a decision had been reached, the battle began by the National [Union] troops firing on the enemy. . . .

I do not question the personal courage of General Johnston, or his ability. But he did not win the distinction predicted for him by many of his friends. He did prove as a general he was over-estimated."

Union troops accept the surrender of Confederates in New Mexico.

ville, destroying two railroad bridges in the process. Union troops were then detached to patrol the railroad and to find Forrest.

PERRYVILLE

As a result of these cavalry raids, Buell's Chattanooga campaign stalled. He was soon drawn into Kentucky when Confederate general Braxton Bragg invaded that state in late August. Bragg was to be one of the most controversial figures of the war. A strict disciplinarian, who believed in absolute observance of regulations, his campaigns often started well but failed because he was unable to see them through to the end.

Bragg found little resistance in the early days of his invasion. However, on October 8, part of Buell's command ran into some of Bragg's at Perryville, Kentucky. Fighting soon erupted. Neither Buell nor Bragg committed all of his troops to the fight: Buell because he was unaware of the extent of the fighting until late afternoon and Bragg because his troops were too scattered.

By sunset, the Confederates had pushed the Union back a mile, but instead of continuing the battle the next day, Bragg retreated back into Tennessee. In part, the Confederate general feared that he was vastly outnumbered. But also, as Foote notes, his action was based "on an overrating of Buell, who he thought would press him hard, and an underrating of his own troops."[33]

Despite his victory, Buell was in trouble with his superiors because he failed to pursue the retreating enemy, letting Bragg quietly slip back over the Ten-

his main supply base, Louisville, Kentucky.

Meanwhile, on July 13, Forrest, a plantation owner and a former slave trader known as "Old Bedford," rode fifty miles in fourteen hours and overran Murfreesboro, Tennessee. He captured Union general Thomas T. Crittenden and his entire command, as well as a million dollars' worth of supplies. The raiders later attacked Lebanon, Tennessee, and chased the retreating Federal garrison to Nash-

nessee border. Ultimately, he was relieved of his command, although his actions at Perryville ended any serious Confederate threat to Kentucky.

WILLIAM TECUMSEH SHERMAN

By late fall, Grant was in command in the West because Halleck had left for Washington to become the new army commander in chief. On November 27, Grant began a campaign he hoped would win him Vicksburg. He planned first to capture Jackson, Mississippi. From there, he would be able to safely march due west to Vicksburg. At the same time, General William T. Sherman was to take the high grounds to the northeast of Vicksburg.

Sherman had graduated sixth in his 1840 West Point class and served in California during the Mexican War. Resigning from the army in 1854, he eventually became a superintendent of a Louisiana military academy. When Louisiana seceded, he moved on to become president of a St. Louis streetcar company before rejoining the army as a colonel in May 1861.

PASSING THE TIME

When not in combat, the soldiers of both sides found ways of combating the boredom of camp life, as seen in this excerpt from Confederate Bromfield Ridley's 1906 war memoir, Battles and Sketches of the Army of Tennessee, *found in* The Civil War Archive, *edited by Henry Steele Commager:*

"The guards around a regiment halloo out [yell out], 'T-w-e-l-v-e o'-c-l-o-c-k and a-l-l-'s well!' The rude . . . soldier would play on that and say: 'T-w-e-l-v-e o'-c-l-o-c-k and sleepy as hell!' . . . Let a stranger or soldier enter camp and call for a certain company—say, Company F. Some soldier will say, 'Here's Company F!' By the time he can get there, another will cry out at the far part of the regiment, 'Here's Company F!' Then the whole command will take up the refrain, until the poor fellow in vexation will sulk away. . . .

In the army we have some of the finest mimics in the world. Let one cackle like a hen, . . . then other cacklers take it up, until it sounds like a poultry yard stirred up by over a mink or weasel. . . . As mimics they are perfect; as musicians, also. . . . I met one . . . [who] put his hands to his chin, and with his teeth made a sound like rattling bones, keeping time to his . . . song. Some of the finest singers I ever heard were soldiers and some of the best acting I ever saw was done by them."

Sherman had performed ably at the first Bull Run and was promoted to brigadier general and posted to Kentucky. There, however, he overestimated Confederate troop buildup in eastern Tennessee and suddenly called off an invasion of the region. He was then transferred to a minor assignment in Missouri.

Sherman's career was reborn when he was called upon to supply reinforcements for Grant's Forts Henry and Donelson campaign. The two men worked well together, and Sherman, although the military senior of the two, agreed to serve under Grant.

YEAR'S END

The Vicksburg campaign did not go well. On December 20, Confederate cavalry destroyed Grant's supply base at Holly Springs, Mississippi, and the Northern general was forced to fall back to Memphis. Sherman, unaware of Grant's retreat, but still expecting his assistance in an assault on Vicksburg, continued his advance. He was stopped at the bloody battle of Chickasaw Bayou on December 29. He later wrote:

> General Grant . . . had sent me word of the change [his retreat], but it did not reach me in time; indeed, I was not aware of it until after my assault. . . . There was no bungling on my part, for I never worked harder or with more intensity of purpose in my life; and General Grant, long after, . . . gave us all full credit for the skill of the movement, and described the almost impregnable [unconquerable] nature of the ground.[34]

General Braxton Bragg led the Confederates in a strong offensive campaign in Kentucky.

REACTION TO DEFEAT

Many Confederate soldiers in the western theater were discouraged by the series of defeats their command suffered, as seen in the first two letters below by S.B. Thornbrough and W.W. Grissam, reprinted in The Brothers' War, *edited by Annette Tapert. However, others, such as William Nugent, author of the third letter, found in Steven E. Woodworth's* Cultures in Conflict, *were more optimistic.*

I heard today that the south had given Nashville up without the fire of a gun and retreated back to Memphis and if that be so I fear it will be a hard struggle for us and probably one that will prove to be a death stroke to the . . . Confederacy.

Half of the male hands [slaves] in all this country have been sent to fortify No. 10 [Confederate stronghold on the Mississippi River] but I am afraid that it will be of no avail. I learn that New Madrid [Missouri] is in the possession of the enemy, and will they not cut off our supplies by river?

While we have had reverses, we have had successes. Sleeping upon a fancied security at New Orleans we were suddenly aroused . . . and are being taught the hourly lesson . . . [of] ceaseless watchfulness. In fact we needed some lessons that only defeats could teach us. Men learn nothing but by experience, and nations composed of aggregated individuals labor under the same infirmity.

The Union received two other rough blows in the West during December. Morgan's raiders once more ransacked central Kentucky, destroying some $2 million of Federal property and capturing almost two thousand prisoners. And, beginning on December 31 and continuing for three days, at Stones River, near Murfreesboro, Tennessee, Confederate and Union forces hammered mercilessly at each other, resulting in twelve thousand casualties on each side. The battle ended in a technical victory for the Federals when the Southerners left the battlefield on January 2, but the Union army was so weakened that it would not take to the field again for another six months.

The Union had scored an impressive series of victories in the western campaign of 1862. However, the grim ending of the year, although it had little effect on the overall course of the war, combined with the despair over eastern defeats to cast gloom over the North.

5 1863: The Home Fronts

As 1863 opened, the momentum of victory seemed to be with the Confederacy, despite its overall poor showing in the West. Fredericksburg and other recent Union setbacks had hit the North like hammer blows. To the South, they were the heralds of independence. Yet, whether their citizens were pessimistic or optimistic about the final outcome of the war, both North and South had political and domestic problems to face.

DARK TIMES FOR THE UNION

The war news remained grim for the North in the early months of 1863. On January 20, an attempt by Burnside to move around Lee's army ended when heavy rain turned the Virginia roads to mud. Six days later, Lincoln named General Joseph Hooker as commander of the Army of the Potomac and reassigned Burnside to Ohio. In the West, Grant, though still firmly in command, seemed equally mired in failure after his Vicksburg campaign stalled.

Frustration at the Union's inability to smash the Confederacy mounted in the North as the war dragged into its third year. Union morale was at an all-time low. Many in the North were growing tired of the conflict, particularly the staggering death toll of combat. Even the most patriotic had come to doubt that the Union could win the war. The *Chicago Tribune* summarized this despair:

> Failure of the army, weight of taxes, depreciation of money, want of cotton, . . . increasing national debt, deaths in the army, no prospect of success, the continued closure of the Mississippi [River] . . . all combine to produce the existing state of despondency and desperation. . . . The war is drawing toward a disastrous and disgraceful termination.[35]

This same gloom also ran through the Northern army. "The army is tired with its hard and terrible experience," wrote Captain Oliver Wendell Holmes Jr., while recovering from his second wound of the conflict. "I've pretty much made up my mind that the South has achieved their independence."[36] The Confederacy's strategy of wearing down the North seemed to be working.

CABINET CRISIS

The blame for the Union troubles fell squarely on Lincoln. Friends and foes alike explained Federal failure by criticizing everything about the president, including his decision making, his policy, his character, and even his physical appearance.

Realizing there was little that could be done about Lincoln until the 1864 election, Republican senators recommended strengthening the White House by reorganizing the cabinet. The major change was to be the removal of Secretary of State William Seward, one of the president's closest advisors. Secretary of the Treasury Salmon P. Chase, a political enemy of Seward, claimed that the secretary of state's influence was to blame for the lackluster prosecution of the war.

NEW JERSEY OPPOSES THE WAR

As the war dragged into its third year and Northern losses in the East mounted, opposition to the war effort arose. In early 1863 the New Jersey legislature passed a resolution, reprinted in The Civil War Archive, *edited by Henry Steele Commager, protesting the continuance of hostilities:*

"Be It Resolved by the Senate and General Assembly of the State of New Jersey, . . . [we] make unto the Federal government this our solemn Protest

Against a war waged with the insurgent [rebellious] States for . . . accomplishment of unconstitutional or partisan purposes;

Against a war which has for its object the subjugation of any of the States, with their view to the reduction of their territorial condition; . . .

Against the domination of the military over the civil laws in States, Territories, or districts not in a state of insurrection;

Against all arrests without warrants . . . ;

Against the power assumed in the [Emancipation] proclamation of the President . . .

Against any and every exercise of power upon the part of the Federal Government that is not clearly given and expressed by the . . . Constitution. . . .

And be it Resolved, That while abating naught in her devotion to the Union of the States and the dignity and power of the Federal Government, at no time since the commencement of the present war has this State been other than willing to terminate peacefully and honorably to all war unnecessary in its origin, fraught with horror and suffering in its prosecution, and necessarily dangerous to the liberties of all in its continuation."

Secretary of State William Seward (second, right) almost resigned when Republican party leaders complained about him to President Abraham Lincoln (left).

To deal with this political crisis, Lincoln met with the senators and listened to their complaints about Seward, who unknown to them had offered to resign if it would defuse the situation. The next day, the president invited the lawmakers to meet with his entire cabinet, minus the secretary of state. He told the visitors that every one of his cabinet members had approved all major policy decisions, and even Chase was forced to admit that this was true. Unable to find any evidence of Seward's supposed influence over Lincoln, the senators retracted their demands for the secretary of state's removal.

COPPERHEADS

Among Lincoln's most vocal opponents were members of a growing peace movement. Some of these antiwar Northerners were members of the Democratic Party. To distinguish themselves from Democrats who supported the war, they called themselves Peace Democrats. To their Republican enemies, they were Copperheads, named for a venomous snake that people in the nineteenth century thought was tricky and struck without warning. According to Neely, Copperheads were a minority in the Democratic Party. Like Republicans, most Democrats were fully committed to reuniting the country:

Though critical [of the president] the Democrats remained loyal [to the Union]. During the war . . . it was commonly believed that there were vast organizations in the North whose members were disloyal Democrats, . . . the Copperheads. . . . The Copperhead menace was wildly exaggerated by Republican fears; the Democratic party constituted a loyal opposition.[37]

The peace movement demanded an instant end to the war even if peace meant recognizing the Confederacy as a separate nation, although some Peace Democrats claimed, without any evidence, that the Southern states would rejoin the Union once the fighting ceased. In any case, for members of the peace movement, the whole idea of a restored Union was an abstraction not worth throwing lives away for.

One of the most outspoken Copperheads was Clement L. Vallandigham, a former Democratic congressman who planned to run for governor of his home state of Ohio. Vallandigham was a dynamic speaker who missed no opportunity to condemn both the war and Lincoln and to champion slavery and states' rights.

HABEAS CORPUS

Vallandigham and other Peace Democrats had many complaints about Lincoln's leadership. They were particularly critical of the president's suspension of the writ of habeas corpus, a constitutional protection against unlawful arrest and detainment. Habeas corpus requires that any person arrested be brought before a regular court to hear charges and

then be tried in that court by a jury, or the arrestee must be released.

The Constitution provides for suspension of habeas corpus in times of invasion or rebellion. It is unclear, however, who has the authority to order that suspension: the president, the Congress, or the two acting together. In any case, Lincoln had suspended the writ for anyone thought guilty of treason. Such people could, therefore, be arrested, tried by the military, and imprisoned or executed. Indeed, such suspects might even be held indefinitely without trial. Before the war was over, several hundred people found themselves under military arrest. One of them was Clement L. Vallandigham.

On May 5, 1863, Burnside, irritated by Vallandigham's constant railing against the war, had him arrested, tried by a military tribunal, and thrown into prison. Lincoln, who only learned of the arrest when he read of it in the newspaper, was embarrassed by the incident since it looked as though he were using presidential powers to eliminate his political foes. At the same time, he did not wish to undermine military authority. Thus, the president commuted Vallandigham's sentence to exile and had him put across the border into Confederate territory. The exiled politician eventually gained passage on a blockade runner that took him to Canada. From there he continued campaigning—unsuccessfully—for the Ohio governorship.

THE DRAFT

Peace Democrats and others also attacked another wartime measure: the draft, or conscription. Initially, after the

FARM WOMEN

"Frequent calls of business took me through the extensive farming districts of Wisconsin, and Eastern Iowa. . . . As we dashed along the railway, . . . it took us through what seemed a continuous wheat-field. . . .

Women were in the field everywhere, driving the reapers, binding . . . and loading grain. . . . At first, it displeased me, and I turned away in aversion. By and by, I observed how skillfully they drove the horses round and round the wheat-field. . . .

One day my route took me off the railway, . . . and the carriage stopped opposite a field where half a dozen women and two men were harvesting. . . . I walked over and accosted them. . . .

'And so you are helping gather the harvest!' I said to a woman. . . . 'Yes, ma'am,' she said, 'the men have all gone to the war, so that my man can't hire help at any price, and I told my girls we must turn to and give him a lift.' . . .

'Have you sons in the army?'

'Yes,' and a shadow fell over the motherly face. . . . 'All three of 'em 'listed [enlisted], and Neddy, the youngest was killed.' . . .

Further conversation disclosed the fact that amid their double labor in the house and field, these women found time for the manufacture of hospital supplies, and had helped fill box after box with shirts . . . , dried apples and pickles, currant wine and blackberry jam, to be forwarded to the poor fellows . . . in far-off . . . hospitals."

shelling of Fort Sumter, volunteers appeared by the tens of thousands. Indeed, they overwhelmed the resources of the North, which did not have the uniforms, weapons, or equipment to field so many enthusiastic would-be soldiers. Later, however, matters changed drastically. As the war dragged on and casualties mounted, men became reluctant to enlist. Thus, the Union had to resort to the draft, the forceful recruitment of soldiers, to fill the ranks of their armies.

On March 3, 1863, Congress passed, and Lincoln later signed, the Federal

Conscription Act. Numerous loopholes, however, allowed many to escape the draft. For instance, a draftee could pay a $300 fee to be excused from conscription. Another allowable practice was paying a substitute to enter the army in a draftee's place. Consequently, many wealthy men avoided military service, leading to the charge that it was "a rich man's war and a poor man's fight."[38]

THE NEW YORK DRAFT RIOT

This unequal treatment of draftees created much bitterness and, on Sunday, July 12, 1863, led to a riot in New York City. The rioters were workers who were angry about being drafted. They hated the war because of its goal of freeing the slaves in the South. The rioters believed that they would lose their jobs to these freed blacks since the wages of African Americans were lower than those of other workers.

For four days, mobs of angry men and women roamed the streets. They burned Federal buildings, particularly draft offices. They attacked any newspaper office, such as that of the *New York Tribune*, that supported the war.

African Americans were also targets of the rioters. The mobs lynched half a dozen blacks and beat up many more. They wrecked black homes and property and even burned one African American orphanage to the ground.

The New York police force, unable to control the rioting, asked the army for

At the start of the war, volunteers line up outside a recruiting office to join the Union army.

On July 12, 1863, rioters in New York City go on a rampage of arson and looting in reaction to the Federal Conscription Act.

help. Several regiments were ordered to New York, arriving on July 15. The soldiers, veteran combat troops, opened fire on the rioters. Within a day of the military's arrival, the riots were over. The final death toll was well over a hundred.

DAVIS UNDER ATTACK

Unlike in the North, general support for the war remained strong in the South. Southerners, like Northerners, were disturbed by the bloody cost of battle, but they saw it as a necessary price to be paid to save their homes and families from invasion.

Many of them were less happy with the progress of the war and, in particular, with Confederate president Jefferson Davis. Indeed, a vocal set of critics in the Confederate Congress believed that Davis

was unfit to govern. His many conflicts with generals, cabinet members, and even his vice president provided much ammunition for his opponents. Also, many were unhappy with the manner in which the western Confederacy was deprived of troops and resources in favor of Virginia. Still others disliked the conscription act that Davis had pushed through the Confederate Congress in 1862; the slaughter of battle had also slowed the volunteer rate in the South and left the army desperate for soldiers. As with the Northern act, a draftee could buy his way out, giving rise to the same complaint that poor men were forced to fight for the interests of rich men.

Davis's critics further pointed out that Davis was unable to delegate authority: He often dealt with matters that should have been assigned to others. William C. Davis writes:

He passed his . . . eye over seemingly every document—passes and transfers, promotions and assignments, complaints of every description, and even minor civil matters. . . . Much was directed at the president by mistake. . . . But instead of reforming the inefficiency, he encouraged it. Indeed, despite his protestations of the burden of this work, Davis, ever the bureaucrat, clearly enjoyed it.[39]

As a consequence, Davis's own presidential duties were frequently obscured or lost in the mass of paperwork that crossed his desk.

THE CONFEDERATE NATION

Part of the discontent with Davis stemmed from a fear that the national government was growing too strong at the expense of the Confederacy's member states. Indeed,

---

HARD TIMES IN LITTLE ROCK

In the following letter, found in Cultures in Conflict, *edited by Steven E. Woodworth, Union supporter and Southern resident Eliza Wilcox Graves painted a grim portrait of wartime civilian life in late 1862 Little Rock, Arkansas:*

"We have come out from Rebeldom, escaped as it were by the 'skin of our teeth.' We were over three years in Little Rock fast stuck in and under such military discipline by Gen[eral] [Thomas] Hindman's & Gen. [Sterling] Price's orders that we could not write or receive letters, newspapers, etcetera for nearly two years except some came through by private soldiers subject if found out to severe discipline. Every article of food or clothing was very scarce. We paid 25 dollars for a pound of tea . . . , $150 for the last two barrels of Flour we purchased, . . . and everything else accordingly. . . .

We were Union all the time but dare not say one word even to ourselves. For you know in Arkansas neither Law or Gospel has much influence when the voice of some few people . . . can call together enough to take Lynch law into their hands. . . . When we saw a gentleman of our acquaintance one hour we almost ceased to be surprised if the next one came to tell us he had been assassinated in his house or on the street. It became to us . . . a time of horror. . . . [After escaping] we travelled in ironclad [railroad] cars and were in constant danger from Guerrillas . . . and incendiaries on board the steamboats on the river until we reached Cairo [Illinois]."

Overcoming Shortfalls

"As no shoe . . . polish could be bought during the blockade, each family improvised its own blacking, which was soot and oil of some variety . . . mixed together. The shoes would be well painted with the mixture. . . . Then a thin paste of flour . . . was applied all over the blackened shoe . . . , which paste, when dry, gave the shoe as bright and glossy an appearance as if 'shined.' . . .

The obtaining of salt became extremely difficult. . . . All the brine [salt water] left in . . . barrels, where pork had been salted down, was carefully dipped up, boiled down, and converted into salt again. In some cases the salty soil under old smoke-houses [where meat was preserved] was dug up and placed in hoppers [containers that opened at the bottom]. . . . Water was then poured upon the soil, the brine which percolated [moved] through the hopper was boiled down to the proper point, poured into vessels, and set in the sun, which by evaporation completed the . . . process. Though never of immaculate whiteness, the salt which resulted from these methods served well enough . . . , and we accepted it without complaining. . . .

One of our most difficult tasks was to find a good substitute for coffee. . . . [Some] saved a few handfuls of coffee, and used it on very important occasions, and then only as an extract . . . for flavoring substitutes for coffee. . . . The seeds [of okra], when mature and nicely browned, came nearer the flavor to the real coffee than any other substitute. . . . Yam potatoes . . . were thought to be next best. . . . Browned wheat, meal, and burnt corn made passable beverages."

Davis was often accused of being a despot and a dictator, accusations also leveled at Lincoln. To some extent, these charges were true since Davis did make unilateral decisions, not even consulting his cabinet, let alone the Confederate Congress or the various state governors. And yet, the crises of war did not always permit such consultations.

In any case, two years of war had changed the Confederacy more than its founders could have foreseen. To wage a full-scale war, each state had had to give up some of its powers to the central government. Additionally, the rugged individualism valued by Southerners had had to be sacrificed—at least in part—to the war effort. According to Thomas,

> The organization necessary to armies and the war government necessarily circumscribed [restricted] Southerners' vaunted [prized] individualism. . . . The discipline inherent in the organization of mass armies and the regimentation involved in governmental functions such as conscription, taxation, [and] martial law . . . set limits on the sphere within which Southerners could exercise their individualism.[40]

SHORTAGES AND INFLATION

Other factors also chipped away at the old Southern way of life. Among these were shortages; the Confederate states were running short of supplies, including guns, clothes, and food. The South's few factories could not keep up with the demands of war, and growing enough food was a problem because much of the best Southern farmland was occupied by Union troops. Bringing in enough supplies and food from other countries was impossible because of the Federal naval blockade. Additionally, Confederate money was practically worthless, and inflation ran as high as 9,000 percent. Prices soared, and even when goods and food were available, few could afford them.

Rich and poor were finding life in the South increasingly difficult. Not only were the fine foods and fancy clothes of the wealthy hard to come by, but so were necessities. A clerk in the Confederate War Department in Richmond wrote that "famine is upon us. I have lost twenty pounds, and my wife and children are emaciated [very thin]."[41]

WARRIORS AND SLAVES

It was thus hard to maintain the old Southern aristocratic ideals in the face of the realities of war. Success often meant more than breeding. The greatest Confederate war hero was the grim, puritanical Stonewall

Stonewall Jackson, seen here in 1860, was the greatest Confederate war hero.

Jackson, not the flamboyant cavalier Jeb Stuart or the aristocratic Robert E. Lee.

Still, in one important way, the South of 1863 was the same as that of the past: Slavery remained. On paper, Lincoln's Emancipation Proclamation set free African Americans in the Confederacy. But in reality, it did nothing. Black slaves worked the fields, they built the military installations, they delivered supplies, and they even worked as nurses in hospitals. Their labor freed up many white Southerners for army duty.

The Confederacy's two years of existence were too short a time to have allowed a national character to develop, particularly while fighting a fierce war for survival. Still, in the winter and spring of 1863, it appeared to most Southerners—and to many Northerners—that the South would soon win its independence and have an opportunity to evolve into a society different from that of the United States. This outlook would change drastically come the summer.

Chapter 6

1863: Turning Points

As the war dragged on, both sides desperately wanted victories. The Lincoln administration needed to show dispirited Northerners that the Union could win the war, and Davis and Lee needed a decisive victory that would destroy the North's ability to wage war. Thus, in June 1863, Lee once more invaded the Union, looking to change the course of the war, while besieged Confederates grimly hung on in the West in Vicksburg.

To Outmaneuver Lee

The new commander of the Army of the Potomac, Joseph Hooker, was a tough, smart veteran combat officer who had done well in the Peninsula campaign and at Antietam and Fredericksburg. Upon taking command, Hooker immediately rebuilt the morale of the badly battered Union army. He handed out leaves of absence, issued food and clothing, and created insignia for each army division. Reinforcements filled the ranks until the army numbered 115,000.

Lee's Army of Northern Virginia still occupied the heights above Fredericksburg, but Hooker had no intention of a frontal assault like that ordered by Burnside. Instead, he planned to catch Lee

between two converging Union forces. So, on April 27, leaving some ten thousand soldiers at Fredericksburg to mount a diversionary attack against the Confederates, Hooker took most of his troops several miles along the Rappahannock and then across it. On April 30, the Northern general set up his headquarters at Chancellorsville, a village some nine miles west of Fredericksburg in the middle of a tangle of trees and brush known as the Wilderness.

Informed of Hooker's position by Jeb Stuart's cavalry, Lee marched to Chancellorsville. He left part of his army at Fredericksburg to fight the Federals there, giving him forty-two thousand against more than two and half times that many enemy. He then further divided his troops, sending Stonewall Jackson with some twenty-eight thousand men on a forced march to outflank Hooker. With the tiny remainder, Lee hit Hooker on the morning of May 2.

Chancellorsville

Unnerved by the Confederate attack, Hooker ordered his men to dig in. The day passed with Lee keeping the pressure on Hooker. Then, two hours before sunset, Jackson's troops burst out of the Wilderness, taking the Federals completely by surprise. In one of the few night actions of the war, the two armies fought a fierce battle that sometimes had troops firing at their own side by mistake in the dark.

One of the casualties of friendly fire was Jackson, who, while riding to inspect the Confederate lines, was shot by his own men. Later that night, surgeons amputated the general's arm at the shoulder in an effort to save his life. Jeb Stuart temporarily took over Jackson's troops and

A stained glass window honors Robert E. Lee, depicted on his horse, shaking hands with a soldier.

led them in heavy fighting the next day. Military scholar Thomas B. Buell writes:

> Once again the Confederates' aggressiveness caused the Federal command to flinch. Hooker withdrew . . . , uncovering the road that allowed Lee to reunite both wings of his assault force. As a further gift to Lee, Hooker abandoned the high ground at Fairview Hill, which the Confederate artillery immediately occupied to bombard the contracting Federal lines.[42]

Only news that the Federals at Fredericksburg had broken through the Confederate defense stopped Lee's attack. The Southern general immediately set off and pushed the breakout Union troops back across the Rappahannock. He then returned to Chancellorsville on May 6, only to find Hooker had also crossed the river.

THE GRAVEST LOSS OF ALL

Chancellorsville was a brilliant victory for Lee, who with masterful and daring tactics defeated a far better equipped and numerically superior foe. However, the price was high; fourteen thousand Confederates were dead and wounded, a quarter of the Army of Northern Virginia. But the single gravest loss was Stonewall Jackson, who, weakened by the amputation of his arm, contracted pneumonia and died on May 10. The news of the general's death shocked the South. According to Robertson:

> The Southern nation had to weather the greatest personal loss it would ever know. Jackson's passing was tragedy in its purest form. The effect

A family tends to an injured Confederate soldier wounded in battle at Chancellorsville.

on the civilian population could only be called paralyzing. . . . A Richmond newspaper did not exaggerate when it proclaimed: "The affections of every household in the nation were twined about this great and unselfish warrior. . . . He had fallen and a nation weeps."[43]

Even Lee wept when he heard the news that the man he called his right arm was dead. He admitted to his son Custis that he had no idea how to replace Jackson. He could only promote General Richard S. Ewell, Jackson's second in command, to head the dead general's corps. Ewell was a competent officer, but no one, including Ewell, thought him to be in a league with Stonewall.

INVASION PLAN

No matter how glorious a victory Chancellorsville had been, it had not come close to dealing a death blow to the Army of the Potomac, even though Union casualties had been seventeen thousand. The Union ranks were again filled, and as Federal general Abner Doubleday later wrote, "the Union army [was] still strong and ready, as soon as reinforcements and supplies arrived. . . . Our army . . . was still [too] formidable in numbers . . . to be effectively assailed [attacked]. . . . The Rebels had obtained a triumph rather than a substantial victory at Chancellorsville."[44]

Lee knew he was running out of time. He was short of men and supplies, and shortages of both were only going to get worse. He had to land a knockout punch and do it quickly. And he thought the best place to do so was Pennsylvania, deep in Union territory.

Lee's plan was to lure the Army of the Potomac north, where he would force the Federal army into battle. He had absolute confidence that he and his men could win, particularly after Fredericksburg and Chancellorsville. And this time, he would crush the Army of the Potomac.

A victorious Southern army would then be in a position to threaten not only Washington, but also Baltimore and Philadelphia. Ultimately, the North would have no choice but to negotiate a peace.

On to Pennsylvania

On June 3, all of Lee's preparations were made, and he took the Army of Northern Virginia west to the Shenandoah Valley, along which he planned to head north. Eleven days later, Ewell's corps attacked and drove off the Union garrison at Winchester, Virginia, leaving the way north clear. On June 15, the Army of Northern Virginia once more crossed the Potomac into Maryland.

Meanwhile, Hooker, believing that Lee's intention was to attack the Army of the Potomac from the rear, stayed on the Rappahannock. On June 13, receiving word of Ewell's presence at Winchester, the Federal general started his troops north, keeping them between Lee and Washington.

A New Commander

The first Confederates reached Pennsylvania on June 24; Lee arrived two days later. The Southern commander intended to supply his troops from Northern towns and farms and thus let his army spread out so that the various units could seek provisions and equipment over as wide an area as possible. Among other things, the Southern soldiers gathered food, medicine, horse equipment, and clothes. They also took every healthy horse they found, a number that totaled in the thousands.

Union cavalry reported that the Army of Northern Virginia was strung out along its march route, and Lincoln suggested to Hooker that the Union commander attack Lee's force and cut it in two. Hooker refused, saying that he could not attack because he was sure that he was outnumbered. In fact the Army of Northern Virginia was, as usual, considerably smaller than the Army of the Potomac. On June 28, his patience exhausted with Hooker, Lincoln replaced him with General George G. Meade, who had led his troops well even at such major Union defeats as Fredericksburg and Chancellorsville.

Rendezvous at Gettysburg

Meade quickly marched his army north, stopping just short of the Pennsylvania border at Pipe Creek, near Taneytown, Maryland. He ordered his cavalry to spread out into Pennsylvania and find the Army of Northern Virginia. Meanwhile, Lee settled himself at Chambersburg, Pennsylvania.

The two armies collided at Gettysburg, Pennsylvania, some twenty-two miles from Chambersburg and twelve from Pipe Creek. On the evening of June 30, Confederates investigating a rumor that Gettysburg contained a supply of shoes ran into Union cavalry and quickly retreated.

Refuge on Cemetery Hill

Commanded by Kentucky-born general John Buford, the Federals at Gettysburg called for reinforcements and then prepared for a Confederate attack, which came early on July 1. The fighting was

PICKETT'S CHARGE

Union soldier Warren Goss in his 1890 Recollections of a Private, *excerpted in* Voices of the Civil War, *edited by Richard Wheeler, described the famous and doomed charge of Confederate general George Pickett's division on the final day at Gettysburg:*

"[Pickett's men] came on in magnificent order, with the step of men who believed themselves invincible. . . . A light wind sprang up, and the smoke of their guns [artillery] drifted over the valley. . . . For a moment it threatened to obscure the charging columns from the sight of those who were about to encounter them in the grapple of death. . . . The smoke drifted lazily away . . . , revealing to us the gray lines steadily advancing. . . .

Solid shot ploughs huge lanes in their close columns. As the enemy approach still nearer, shells burst upon their compact masses. Their shattered lines do not waver, but steadily closing up the gaps of death, come on in magnificent order. With banners waving, with steady step, they sweep on like an irresistible wave of fate. . . .

The Union soldiers . . . clutch their muskets. . . . On come the rebel lines with bayonets glistening. . . . Now the Union guns [artillery] open up . . . at close range upon this line of human targets. . . . As they come on, they leave behind them a trail of dead and dying. . . .

Now they are at . . . musket range, and from behind the stone wall a wave of flame, perceivable even in the noonday light, springs from the muzzles of the line of Union muskets. Volley after volley is poured in with deadly effect upon them."

fierce and heavy; the Confederates finally broke through the Union line in late afternoon. After a running fire fight through the town, the Federals retreated to the top of nearby Cemetery Hill, where they began digging trenches, and to adjacent Culp's Hill. The two heights were connected by a land bridge.

Lee arrived on the battlefield in the afternoon and, after watching the Federal retreat, decided to make Gettysburg the site of his major offensive against Meade. The Confederate commander ordered Ewell to attack Cemetery Hill before the Union troops could finish preparing their defenses. However, Ewell decided such an assault would be foolhardy. The Federal position was too strong, and Cemetery Hill was too steep to scale in the face of firm resistance, particularly for soldiers tired from the day's hard fighting.

THE DEVIL'S DEN AND THE ROUND TOPS

Meade arrived at Gettysburg just before dawn on July 2. Keeping troops on the two hills, he spread a line of Union soldiers south along a high rise, known as Cemetery Ridge, that projected from Cemetery Hill. A mile west, the Confederates occupied a parallel formation, Seminary Ridge.

At noon, Lee began positioning his troops for an attack on the Federal position. In late afternoon, the Confederates surged forward. Deadly fighting erupted along Cemetery Ridge; some of the worst took place in a peach orchard just west of the south end and in a jumble of rocks later called the Devil's Den. Confederate units also attempted to take Cemetery and Culp's Hills.

Just south of Cemetery Ridge rose Round Top and Little Round Top, two hills that overlooked the entire Federal line, as well as both Cemetery and Culp's hills. If the Confederates gained the Round Tops, they could mount artillery and blast the Federals out. Beginning around 5:00 P.M., the two sides met atop these mounds in a bloody struggle that finally saw the Union victorious.

Unable to break the Federal line on Cemetery Ridge, the Confederates were forced to retreat as night fell. The attack on Cemetery Hill also failed, but several Southern units managed to occupy part of Culp's Hill.

A RAIN OF SHELLS

The pre-dawn quiet of July 3 was shattered by the boom of Union artillery firing at the Confederates on Culp's Hill. With first light, the Southerners launched an attack at Federal defenders on the hill, but despite a determined effort, by noon,

Union soldiers defend Cemetery Hill against a Confederate charge.

FEEDING A PRISONER

In a letter home, reprinted in The Brothers' War, *edited by Annette Tapert, Confederate captain Henry Owen talked about his encounter with a Union prisoner:*

"After the great battle of Gettysburg, our division had charge of a lot of prisoners . . . for eight days. Our provisions were scarce. . . .

One day . . . I went along the line of sentinels [sentries]. . . . I found a young . . . officer trying to trade off a neat little pocket flask . . . for a half cake of bread. Our soldiers were trying to see how small a piece he would agree to take. . . .

One of my men told me that he knew a house not far off where I could get breakfast. I went and got the yankee [Northern] officer and told him if he would promise not to try to escape I would take him out to breakfast. He readily promised, and away we went . . . together without even a pistol, chattering gaily. . . . We reached the house and got a splendid breakfast. . . .

When we got through, the old lady [of the house] did not want to take my Confederate money. The yankee pulled out a full purse of his green backs [U.S. money] and paid her. He then purchased three dozen biscuits and we jogged along back to camp. He was very thankful for my kindness and wanted me to accept his flask . . . , but I told him I did not charge for favors and that I had only done my duty to my fellow man in distress."

Lee's soldiers had to retreat in the face of overwhelming Union forces.

An hour later, Confederate artillery began a barrage of the Federal center line on Cemetery Ridge, which became a nightmare as a rain of shells and cannon balls hammered at the troops. Union chaplain Alanson A. Haines described the bombardment as "a terrible rain of hundreds of tons of iron missiles . . . hurled through the air. The forests crashed and the rocks were rent [broken] under the terrible hail . . . the smoke was impenetrable [thick] and rolled over the scene of action concealing all."[45] On Cemetery Ridge, the Union soldiers found shelter wherever they could. They burrowed into shallow trenches, crouched behind stone walls, and slid under fallen trees. Hundreds died, and hundreds more were wounded. Reinforcements dashed forward to take the place of the fallen.

PICKETT'S CHARGE

The firing finally ceased after two hours. It was Lee's plan now to have General George Pickett's division rush the battered Union center. Longstreet objected, saying, "The fifteen thousand men who could make successful assault over that field had never been arrayed [collected] for battle."[46] Lee refused to listen to Longstreet and ordered Pickett to proceed in what would come to be known as Pickett's Charge.

Longstreet's prediction proved all too correct. Artillery and rifle fire wounded, maimed, and killed thousands of the advancing Confederates. Few of the soldiers made it to Cemetery Ridge. Of the 850 men of the Twenty-sixth North Carolina Regiment, for example, only two soldiers reached the Union line. Only at a point in the Federal line known as the Angle did Pickett's men come close to breaking through, but hard Federal resistance ended the threat. The Confederate survivors retreated. Pickett had lost half his command.

BACK TO VIRGINIA

Neither army ventured to renew the battle, and on the evening of July 4, Lee began the long march back to Virginia, crossing the Potomac ten days later. Meade, his army too exhausted to attack the retreating Confederates, shadowed the Army of Northern Virginia. On July 24, Lee stopped his troops at Culpeper, Virginia, south of the Rappahannock. Meade set up camp on the opposite side of the river. For the remainder of the year, the two armies feinted, probed, and skirmished but avoided full-scale combat.

With some fifty thousand casualties, Gettysburg proved to be the bloodiest battle of the war and a disaster for Lee. Instead of the great victory he sought, he had found a major defeat and had lost a third of his men in the process. As Colonel William C. Oates of the Fifteenth Alabama Regiment later observed, "He [Lee] was overconfident."[47] Taking full responsibility for the fiasco, Lee offered Jefferson Davis his resignation, but the Confederate president refused it.

VICKSBURG AGAIN

While the Armies of the Potomac and Northern Virginia slugged it out in the east, other Union and Confederate forces continued to vie for control of the Mississippi River. On January 8, Grant launched his second attempt to take Vicksburg by positioning himself and forty thousand soldiers at Milliken's Bend, Louisiana, west of the Mississippi. He planned to use navy gunboats to protect troop transports that would carry his men across the river. His problem was to find a way for the ironclads and the transports to reach his force safely without being shot up by Vicksburg's guns. Also, such a route would be his supply link with the Federal base at Memphis.

For the next three months, Grant tried to make or find a water passage that would bypass the Vicksburg guns. An attempt to dig a canal ended when rising water from winter rains destroyed the work. A project to widen and deepen natural channels north of Milliken's Bend was abandoned because it was taking too much time to make these waterways navigable; tons of mud had to be removed.

The navy gunboats then tried to make their way to the Yazoo River. This river runs east of Vicksburg and parallels the Mississippi, into which the Yazoo empties north of the city. To reach the Yazoo required steaming through a maze of waterways, many of which were so narrow that the gunboats and transports could barely move. Their slowness almost led to their capture by Confederate infantry, but the timely arrival of Sherman (summoned by the naval commander) prevented the loss of the vessels, which then retreated.

RUNNING THE GAUNTLET

In April, Grant decided to have the gunboats and transports, under the command of Admiral David Porter, steam as swiftly as possible past Vicksburg and hope for the best. The fleet would then meet Grant and ferry him and his troops across the Mississippi south of Vicksburg.

The plan was daring, for it would leave Grant operating in enemy territory, cut off from supplies. Additionally, Porter's vessels would be unable to return to their base since they could not hope to run upriver and make it safely past Vicksburg. The current, which would be with them going downriver, would be against them going back, slowing the craft so that they made perfect targets for the city's artillery.

On the night of April 16, the ironclads and transports, their machinery protected by bales of cotton and hay, made the harrowing passage, running fourteen miles under steady enemy fire. According to Musicant:

From the heights above Vicksburg, a calcium flare burst forth, sending shafts of blinding light onto the river, illuminating every vessel as if on a stage. . . . The *Benton* [Porter's flagboat] . . . steamed within a few yards of the wharf batteries, vomiting broadsides as fast as her gunners could fire. Porter could actually see the crashing bricks of collapsing buildings. The flagboat took one hit . . . that went right through her iron and forty inches of oak, taking off the leg of one man and mangling another.[48]

With the loss of only one transport and no one killed and few wounded, the squadron made it past the city.

TO VICKSBURG

On April 30, Grant landed at Bruinsburg, forty miles south of Vicksburg. Within three weeks, in a whirlwind campaign, he won five battles, which included the capture of the Mississippi state capital, Jackson. He also cut off Vicksburg from the army of Joseph Johnston and reached the fortress city itself.

On May 19, Grant, unaware that Vicksburg commander General John Pemberton had recently been reinforced, ordered Sherman to attack the city. Massive rifle and cannon fire from the well-protected Southerners quickly stopped the Union advance, forcing Sherman to retreat. Grant ordered an all-out assault three days later. Land- and ironclad-based cannons bombarded the city, followed by a rush of Federal infantry. Again, the Union troops were beaten back.

THE SIEGE OF VICKSBURG

On May 25, Grant set up a siege of Vicksburg. Although Jefferson Davis sent Johnston seven thousand reinforcements and orders to help the beleaguered city, the Southern general proved too cautious to attack Grant and try to relieve a town that he believed was already lost.

For the next two months, the Vicksburg Confederates and the Federals exchanged artillery fire. By the first days in July, conditions within the city were grim. Low on food, the inhabitants ate horses and dogs, and by some reports, rats. On July 4, Pemberton surrendered the city and his thirty-two thousand troops to Grant.

INSIDE VICKSBURG

In her diary, an unknown writer recorded the following description, excerpted in Voices of the Civil War, *edited by Richard Wheeler, of life in besieged Vicksburg:*

"We are utterly cut off from the world, surrounded by a circle of fire. . . . The fiery shower of shells goes on day and night. . . . People do nothing but eat what they can get, sleep when they can, and dodge the shells. . . . Clothing cannot be washed or anything else done. . . .

The cellar [where they were hiding] is so damp and musty. . . . The confinement is dreadful. . . . I don't know what others do, but we read when I am not scribbling in this. . . .

When the shelling abates, H. [the diarist's husband] goes to . . . get the [newspaper] 'Daily Citizen,' which is still issuing a tiny sheet. . . . It is . . . a rehash of speculations which amuses a half hour. . . .

I am so tired of corn-bread . . . that I eat it with tears in my eyes. We are lucky to get a quart of milk daily from a family near who have a cow they hourly expect to be killed. I send five dollars to market each day, and it buys a small piece of mule meat. . . . It is our custom in the evening to sit in the front room a little while in the dark. . . . H. was at the window and suddenly sprang up, crying, 'Run!' . . . I was just within the door when the crash came that threw me to the floor. . . . Shaken and deafened, I picked myself up. H. had struck a light. I lighted mine. . . . The candles were useless in the dense smoke, and it was many minutes before we could see. Then we found the entire side of the room torn out."

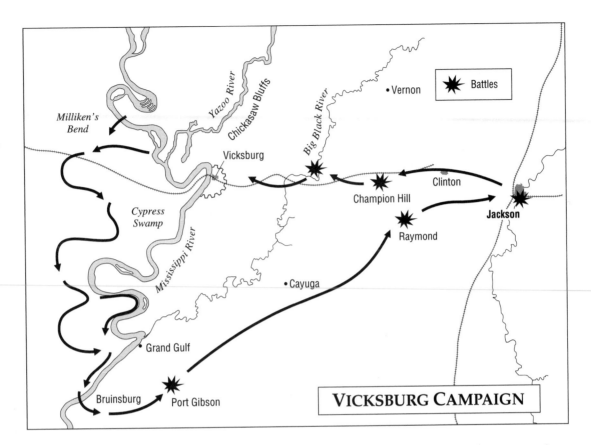

VICKSBURG CAMPAIGN

Five days later, on July 9, Port Hudson, the last Confederate post on the Mississippi, fell. The Union now controlled the entire length of the river, and the far western Southern states were cut off from the East.

THE EFFECT OF GETTYSBURG AND VICKSBURG

The twin defeats of Gettysburg and Vicksburg stunned the South, and Southern morale took a beating. Ultimate Confederate victory no longer seemed assured; as General Josiah Gorgas wrote, "Events have succeeded one another with disastrous rapidity. One month ago we were apparently at the point of success. . . . Now the picture is just as somber as it was bright then. . . . Yesterday we rode on the pinnacle [summit] of success—today absolute ruin seems to be our portion."[49]

In the North, the climate of despair that had gripped the country was suddenly lifted by news of the Union victories. Excitement was everywhere, as bells rang and speeches were made. Of the latter, the most lasting was Lincoln's Gettysburg Address, given at the November 19 dedication of the battlefield as a permanent cemetery for those who had died there. Lincoln summed up the Union's feeling when he said, "It is for us . . . to be dedicated . . . to the great task remaining

Surrender of Vicksburg

On July 4, 1863, Confederate general John Pemberton surrendered Vicksburg to General Ulysses S. Grant, as described by Union soldier George W. Driggs in a letter, reprinted in The Union Reader, *edited by Richard B. Harwell:*

"There had been but little firing during the day previous to the surrender. . . . Gen. Pemberton and staff . . . approached our lines bearing in his hands a flag of truce, which was received by Gen. Grant with all the courtesy due from one high in rank. They met with a smile, each recognizing the other as old class-mates at West Point—shook hands and dismounted, and . . . the two . . . generals proceeded arm in arm to the shade of an old oak tree near by—throwing themselves leisurely upon the grassy ground . . . , they reviewed the past in all kindness and laughed . . . as if they had been daily associates and friends, instead of deadly foes. . . . While Grant sat coolly chewing away upon a stub of a cigar (one of his peculiar traits), Pemberton amused himself pulling up tufts of grass. . . . Pemberton finally broke in on the point of issue, by stating that he . . . had called upon him [Grant] at this time with a view of delivering over the city of Vicksburg—that he had run the thing till the *mule beef* had 'gin out' [given out], and didn't propose to take charge of the place any longer. . . . Grant agreed to relieve him of his command, and after taking a "chaw of tobacco" in unison, they separated to meet again the following day in the city."

Union general Ulysses S. Grant (pictured) accepted the surrender of Confederate general John Pemberton at Vicksburg.

before us . . . that this nation . . . shall have a new birth."[50]

Where at the beginning of 1863, Lincoln had been in deep political trouble, by year's end, his political control was restored. The president's new clout was shown that fall when Republicans swept all the state elections. In Ohio, Peace Democrat Vallandigham lost the governorship by 100,000 votes. Only 6 percent of the Union soldiers supported Vallandigham and his call for an immediate end to the war. The message was clear. The population in the North, both civilian and military, wanted the war to continue.

CHICKAMAUGA

In the fall of 1863, there was more bad news for the South. On September 2, Union troops under Burnside captured Knoxville, Tennessee, and one week later, General William Rosecrans ended a two-month campaign against Bragg. This left the Federals in control of another Tennessee city, Chattanooga.

Flushed with victory, Rosecrans set out in hot pursuit of Bragg, who had retreated just across the border into Georgia. The Northern commander believed that the Confederates were still retreating, but instead, they attacked the Federals on September 19 at Chickamauga Creek.

The force of Bragg's attack broke through part of Rosecrans's line, and a large part of the Union army, their commander included, fled in panic toward Chattanooga. Not all the Northern army fled, however. A section led by General George Thomas stood firm and resisted the Confederate advance, thus allowing the fleeing Federals time to reach Chattanooga safely. For his action, Thomas was named the "Rock of Chickamauga."

ANOTHER DEFEAT

Bragg now posted his men on Lookout Mountain and Missionary Ridge, overlooking Chattanooga. Grant then sent Sherman to join the Chattanooga Federals, led now by Thomas. The Union forces were also joined by units from the Army of the Potomac under the command of Hooker. On November 24, Union troops drove Bragg off Lookout Mountain and, the following day, made a smashing attack on Missionary Ridge that once more sent the Confederate general and his men fleeing into Georgia.

Despite a string of Federal victories, Chickamauga showed the Union that there was still much difficult fighting ahead and that, although the momentum had shifted to the North, the South was far from ready to surrender. Still, the Confederacy would soon face a new challenge: a Union army whose supreme commander was Ulysses S. Grant.

7 1864: The War Continues

As 1864 opened, large chunks of the Confederacy were in Federal hands, and the South was clearly on the defensive. Still, the fight to subdue the Confederacy continued to be tough and costly, particularly in terms of lives. Indeed, the blood toll would be so high that the North's resolve would waver once more.

GENERAL IN CHIEF

On March 9, 1864, Lincoln appointed Grant general in chief of the U.S. Army. The nation's destiny now rested in the hands of a man few had wanted in the military a mere three years before.

As supreme commander, Grant quickly decided on a course of action and set it in motion. Biographer Geoffrey Perret points out:

> [Grant] created a large, mobile army prepared for a war of maneuver. It was free to move in any direction, for any distance, living off the land . . . , and prepared to fight all year round. Its organizing principle was . . . powerful converging columns, designed to apply pressure on the Confederacy from various directions, in season and out, the movements of each col-

umn coordinated with the advance of the rest.[51]

Grant, however, would concentrate most of his resources on defeating the armies of Lee in Virginia and Johnston (who had replaced Bragg) in Georgia since these were the largest Confederate forces in the field. Their loss would open up the Atlantic states of the Confederacy to invasion and conquest. Other Union operations, such as those in Missouri, Mississippi, and Alabama, continued, so that the Confederates had to keep troops in those theaters rather than send them to reinforce Lee and Johnston.

THE WILDERNESS

Grant stationed himself with the Army of the Potomac (which Meade still commanded) and launched his multipronged offensive in mid-spring. On May 4, the 120,000-strong Army of the Potomac moved out of its winter quarters and headed for Richmond. Two days later, Sherman with 100,000 troops began an offensive against Johnston. On May 9, General Philip Sheridan began a series of cavalry raids designed to draw out Jeb Stuart to defeat him. And, on May 15,

General Franz Sigel led a small force of Federals into the Shenandoah Valley to ensure that Confederates did not use it as a base from which to threaten Washington.

In the east, Grant wanted to draw Lee into open-field combat, where the larger, better-armed Northern army could crush the smaller, Southern force, whose sixty thousand troops were outnumbered two to one. Seeking that opportunity, the Army of the Potomac marched into the Wilderness, where a year earlier Hooker had lost the Battle of Chancellorsville. Grant expected the thick forest to hide his movements and was confident he could get his army through this barrier before Lee could respond. This was not to be. Lee learned of Grant's movements from his cavalry scouts and quickly moved the Army of Northern Virginia into the Wilderness. On May 5, the armies clashed, with Grant launching the first attack.

The battle area favored the Southerners since Union artillery and cavalry were useless in the tangled forest and since the jumble of brush and trees made large co-ordinated troop movements impossible. Still, it was not a particularly satisfactory battleground even for the Southerners. Soon small groups of foot soldiers were blundering through the trees, sometimes firing blindly at each other. Fires erupted, burning alive many of the wounded. In the end, after two days of fighting and with eighteen thousand Federal and twelve thousand Confederate casualties; Lee claimed victory.

SPOTSYLVANIA

Instead of retreating as Union commanders had in the past, Grant pressed on, ordering the Army of the Potomac south to the town of Spotsylvania Court House in an attempt to get around Lee. The Confederates raced along parallel roads. On May 8, Southern cavalry delayed the Union advance just long enough for the Army of Northern Virginia to reach a key

General George G. Meade (right), the commander of the Army of the Potomac, directs his cavalry commanders.

MARCHING TO BATTLE

Exhaustion was a common part of both Union and Confederate army life. To reach battle often required long marches, sometimes over inhospitable country. In a letter reprinted in The Brothers' War, *edited by Annette Tapert, Federal sergeant Horatio Newhall talked about the physical toll of one North Carolina campaign:*

"We . . . have been gone ten days, traveled 160 miles for three battles and lived the whole time on hard tack [a thick cracker] and coffee and three days' rations of salt horse. . . . I am so confused in my mind since my return that I can hardly collect my ideas into any kind of shape. . . . My body and mind were at greater strain than ever before *in my life*. . . .

We started on the morning of [December] 11th at six o'clock. . . . We carried more on our backs this time than before, for we had our knapsacks and woolen blankets so that we had quite a load. . . .

The first day we made twelve miles. . . . We were pretty tired for our knapsacks worried our backs plenty. . . . We had had no dinner [lunch] and were hungry. . . .

The next morning we started before daybreak and marched all day without a halt, making eighteen miles and going into camp at ten p.m. . . .

We started the next morning at sunrise and marched through . . . [a] swamp to our knees in water the whole way. . . . The day the advance had skirmishing [fighting] the whole way out. We only made seven miles. . . . We camped on . . . [a] field with the prospect of a fight the next day."

---

crossroads. Here, the Southerners quickly formed a line and fired on the approaching Northerners, who appeared minutes later.

Again, Lee avoided an open-field encounter. Both sides dug entrenchments and threw up temporary fortifications known as breastworks. For the next eleven days, the two armies fought a series of inconclusive but deadly battles. The bloodiest of these affairs was an attack on May 12, in which twenty-two hours of intense fighting left the Federals in control of the Confederate trenches. However, by then Lee had had a new and better line of defense constructed to which the Army of Northern Virginia retreated.

During the struggle at Spotsylvania, word came that, in a nearby May 11 battle with Sheridan's cavalry troopers at a place called Yellow Tavern, Jeb Stuart had been mortally wounded. Lee had lost one of his most valuable officers. Once more, the total casualties for the battle were horrendous.

COLD HARBOR

On May 20, seeing that the two armies were deadlocked at Spotsylvania, Grant took the Army of the Potomac southwest. Again their march was matched by the Army of Northern Virginia. The two forces fought a series of small battles over the next two weeks, with Grant unable to get around Lee and Lee unable to stop Grant.

On June 1, Sheridan's cavalry seized a crossroads named Cold Harbor, just ten miles from Richmond. Both armies raced to the spot, but again the Confederates arrived first, quickly throwing up breastworks and digging trenches. On June 3, impatient with his inability to force Lee into the open, Grant ordered his troops to rush the Confederate fortifications. Fourteen successive waves of Federals failed to overrun Lee's position. Instead the Union soldiers met a deadly wave of rifle and artillery fire. In less than half an hour, seventy-two hundred of Grant's men were wounded or killed.

Grant always regretted the attack at Cold Harbor. In his memoirs he noted, "No advantage was gained to compensate for the heavy loss we sustained. Indeed, the advantages, other than relative losses, were on the Confederate side."[52]

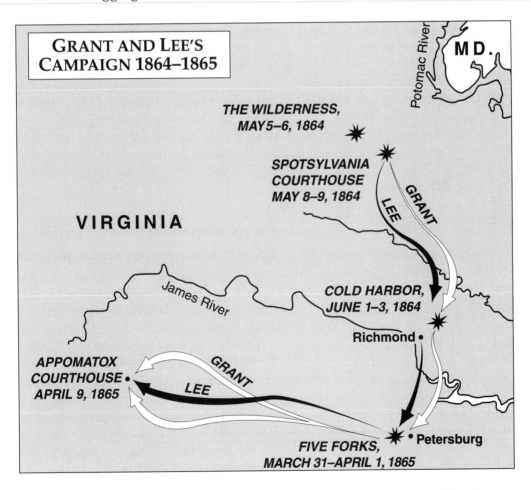

GRANT AND LEE'S CAMPAIGN 1864–1865

Potomac River

MD.

THE WILDERNESS, MAY 5–6, 1864

SPOTSYLVANIA COURTHOUSE MAY 8–9, 1864

LEE

GRANT

VIRGINIA

James River

COLD HARBOR, JUNE 1–3, 1864

Richmond

APPOMATOX COURTHOUSE APRIL 9, 1865

GRANT

LEE

Petersburg

FIVE FORKS, MARCH 31–APRIL 1, 1865

PETERSBURG

On the night of June 12, Grant began moving his troops southeast across the James River for an attack on the railroad hub Petersburg, which was twenty miles south of Richmond and protected only by a small garrison. Large numbers of Union horse soldiers blocked every road, thus ensuring that Lee's now much-depleted cavalry caught no sight of the moving Northern army.

On June 16, Grant began his attack on Petersburg. However, between determined Confederate resistance and poor coordination among the Federal troops, the assault failed. By the evening of June 18, units of the Army of Northern Virginia began to arrive to reinforce the Petersburg defenders.

Using a tactic that had worked at Vicksburg, Grant set up a siege of Petersburg that lasted ten months. During the remainder of 1864, he extended his siege lines so that they threatened the last rail line into Richmond through which a trickle of supplies still reached the Confederate capital and, from there, Lee's men in Petersburg.

THE CRATER

By the beginning of the siege, Grant's total losses for the offensive begun in May were a staggering sixty-five thousand, while Lee's were thirty-seven thousand. Yet, as historian Allan Nevins observes:

Grant had accomplished much. He had bled the South to weakness, especially its échelons of command [senior officers]. He had forced Lee to accept the defensive once and for all. Grant now had a stranglehold on Lee, and by virtue of his tenacity [determination] as well as his superior numbers, was firm in maintaining his iron grip.[53]

Grant ordered continual Union attacks against the Confederate lines to keep the pressure on Lee. One of the most spectacular and least successful of these assaults was the Battle of the Crater. Former Pennsylvania coal miners constructed a five-hundred-foot tunnel, which stretched from beneath the Union lines to just under the Confederate defenses. Then, below the Southern line, the tunnel was packed with thousands of pounds of gunpowder, which was detonated on July 30. The explosion killed some three hundred Confederates and created a huge crater. Union troops then swarmed out of the tunnel into the crater, where bungling Federal leadership and green troops were met by aggressive Southern resistance. The Union soldiers were pushed back and lost four thousand men.

THE SHENANDOAH

Farther west, the Union efforts to clear the Shenandoah Valley of Confederate troops did not go well at first. After routing Federal forces, General Jubal Early thundered through the valley, crossed the Potomac, and arrived at Washington on July 11. The Confederate arrival sent panic through the national capital, whose citizens feared that the city might be captured. However, Washington's defenses plus reinforcements from Grant made it impossible for Early to do any more than light skirmishing. The Southerners soon returned to Virginia.

DEFENDING PETERSBURG

When the advance guard of the Union army reached Petersburg, Virginia, it met a spirited resistance, but not entirely from Confederate regulars, as Anne Bannister related in this selection printed in Cultures in Conflict, *edited by Steven E. Woodworth:*

"There were only a few old men and young boys to defend the town, all the young men being with Lee's army. The sun had risen that morning over the sleepy old town brightly. . . . Suddenly every bell in the town began to toll. . . . Gentlemen and boys ran from their homes to the court house to ascertain what this could mean. In a short while women and children were clustered together to wait and pray for the loved ones, about fifty in number, who armed with nothing but shot-guns, had hastened to the outskirts of the town to try to keep back one thousand raiders. . . . Colonel Archer, hero of the [1848] Mexican War, with his old body servant dragged the small cannon from the public square to the water works where they kept up a constant firing. The constancy of this firing . . . gave . . . the Raiders the impression that it must be a fort. Phil Slaughter, a slave . . . who was a musician, took his little band . . . and played as loudly as possible . . . to make the Yankees think reinforcements were coming. . . . After about two hours of fighting, the Raiders retreated. Twelve of the fifty men and boys were killed. . . . My mother, my sister and I were standing on our porch calling to each one that passed for news from the fight, when my uncle . . . drove up in a wagon with my father's lifeless body shot through the head, his gray hair dabbled in blood."

After defeating another Union army in the valley, Early sent his cavalry back into Union territory to Chambersburg, Pennsylvania, where the Confederates demanded that the townspeople pay for Federal damage in the Shenandoah. When the citizens of Chambersburg refused, the raiders burned the town.

In response, Grant relieved Sheridan of his cavalry duties and sent him to the Shenandoah. The tide now turned. Sheridan beat Early in three different battles in September and October. The Union army then burned the valley's crops, which would have gone to feed Lee's men at Petersburg.

Union general William T. Sherman orders a full assault on Confederate general Joseph Johnston's lines in Georgia.

IN GEORGIA

Meanwhile, Sherman, fresh from his victory at Chattanooga, began his campaign in Georgia. He had two goals: the destruction of Johnston's army and the capture of Atlanta, one of the South's major industrial and transportation centers. Like Lee in Virginia, Johnston had only sixty thousand soldiers and was outnumbered two to one. Unlike Lee, however, Johnston avoided direct battle with his Union foe whenever possible. The Confederate leader's plan was to pick off as many Federals as possible while keeping his own command intact. When Sherman's army was pared down sufficiently, Johnston then planned to attack.

From Sherman's first contact with his opponent on May 9, the pattern for the combat was much the same. The Federals advanced and tried to circle around to attack the Confederates from the rear. Johnston responded with an orderly but quick withdrawal that took both armies deeper into Georgia and closer toward Atlanta. Much of the fighting consisted of small Confederate assaults designed to allow the escape of the main army and which inflicted as many casualties on the enemy as possible.

Hood Takes Command

On July 9, Johnston found himself on the outskirts of Atlanta. Although his own army was almost as strong as ever, his plan to wear down Sherman's army had failed, for reinforcements had refilled the Federal ranks. Thus, on July 17, Jefferson Davis, distrusting Johnston's ability or desire to defend Atlanta, replaced him with John B. Hood, one of the most aggressive generals on either side. Hood believed that the only way to save Atlanta was open battle.

Sherman was delighted with the Confederate command change. The Northern general had the numbers and was confident of victory in any open-field combat. He remarked, "This was just what we wanted, . . . to fight in open ground, on anything like equal terms, instead of being forced to run up against prepared entrenchments."[54]

Hood wasted no time in taking the war to Sherman. On July 20, he attacked the Federals, but only succeeded in losing twenty-five hundred of his own men.

The Price of War

In her diary, Diary from Dixie, *South Carolinian Mary Chesnut wrote of the horrors war held for those who stayed behind:*

"When we read about the battles in India, Italy, the Crimea, what did we care? Only an interesting topic, like any other, to look for in the paper. Now you hear of a battle with a thrill and a shudder. It has come home to us; half the people that we know in the world are under the enemy's guns. A telegram reaches you, and you leave it on your lap. You are pale with fright. You handle it, or you dread to touch it, as you would a rattlesnake; worse, worse, a snake could only strike at you. How many . . . will this scrap of paper tell you have gone to their death? . . .

[Chesnut's friend] Mem Cohen's story to-day. A woman she knew heard that her son was killed, and had hardly taken in the horror of it when they came to say it was all a mistake in the name. She fell on her knees with a shout of joy. . . . The household was totally upset, the swing-back of the pendulum from the scene of weeping and wailing of a few moments before was very exciting. In the midst of this hubbub the hearse drove up with the poor boy in his metallic coffin. . . . Mem's friend is at the point of death . . . ; the sudden changes from grief to joy to grief were more than she could bear."

SHERMAN ON THE CIVIL WAR

Before leaving Atlanta, Sherman ordered the citizens to evacuate the city. The city's mayor protested this order, and in reply, the Union general laid out his feelings about the whole war in a letter, reprinted in Memoirs of William T. Sherman by Himself:

"You cannot qualify war in harsher terms than I will. War is cruelty, and you cannot refine it; and those who brought war into our country deserve all the curses . . . a people can pour out. I know I had no hand in making this war. . . . You cannot have peace and a division of our country. If the United States submits to a division now, it will not stop, but will go on . . . [to] eternal war. . . . Once more acknowledge the authority of the national government, and instead of devoting your houses and streets and roads to the dread use of war, I and this army become at once your protectors and supporters, shielding you from danger, let it come from what quarter it may. . . .

You might as well appeal against the thunder-storm as against these terrible hardships of war. They are inevitable, and the only way the people of Atlanta can hope once more to live in peace and quiet at home, is to stop the war. . . .

I myself have seen . . . hundreds and thousands of women and children fleeing from your armies . . . , hungry and with bleeding feet. . . . Now that war comes home to you, you . . . deprecate its horrors. . . . I want peace, and believe it can only be reached through union and war, and I will ever conduct war with a view toward perfect and early success."

Undaunted, Hood launched another attack two days later. Again he lost, suffering eighty-five hundred casualties. A final assault on July 28 lost Hood another battle and an additional three thousand men.

THE FALL OF ATLANTA

Throughout August, the two sides skirmished. Sherman ordered his artillery to try and blast Hood out of Atlanta, but the bombardment only succeeded in killing civilians. On August 30, Sherman took his army and swung it south of Atlanta. His goal was to cut off the final rail supply link into Atlanta. He was met by Hood, whose command was so weakened that the Federals had no trouble defeating the Confederates.

On September 1, aware that he could no longer hold Atlanta, Hood evacuated his army from the city. The next day, Sherman marched into the city. In total, the two sides had suffered forty thousand casualties in the course of the campaign.

After leaving Atlanta, Hood tried to cut Sherman's supply lines. His attempt failed. Sherman dispatched several units, which drove Hood into Tennessee. There, in a series of ill-advised battles, Hood's army was shattered.

THE NORTH WAVERS

The fall of Atlanta was a much-needed victory for Lincoln, for by the end of the summer of 1864, the president and the Northern war effort were once more in serious trouble. The high casualty rates for both Grant's and Sherman's campaigns shocked the North, and public opinion once more began to shift against

President Abraham Lincoln regained popularity with the fall of Atlanta.

both Lincoln and the war. Cries for a negotiated peace began again.

The presidential election coming in the fall was clearly going to be a referendum on Lincoln and the war. The Republicans at their June convention nominated Lincoln, although a splinter group had formed a third party that nominated its own candidate. However, by late August serious discussion was under way to replace Lincoln as the party nominee.

At the Democratic convention, Peace Democrats, led by Clement Vallandigham, exploited the general air of discontent. To the party platform they added a peace plank promising an immediate ceasefire. They were unsuccessful, however, in getting a peace candidate, and George McClellan became the Democratic nominee.

With the fall of Atlanta, though, Lincoln regained popularity. The news of Sherman's triumph electrified and excited the Northern population, which saw the accomplishment as an assurance of final Union victory. Catton writes, "As the upswing [in public confidence] developed, the move to find a new candidate in place of Lincoln withered. . . . Republicans dutifully lining up behind President Lincoln. . . . Lincoln had a clear road at last."[55] And in the November 8 election, Lincoln easily defeated McClellan.

SHERMAN'S MARCH TO THE SEA

While the Petersburg siege dragged on, Sherman set fire to much of Atlanta. On November 15, he set out for Savannah on the Georgia seacoast. He gave his men leave to forage as they would and destroy anything they could not carry that might

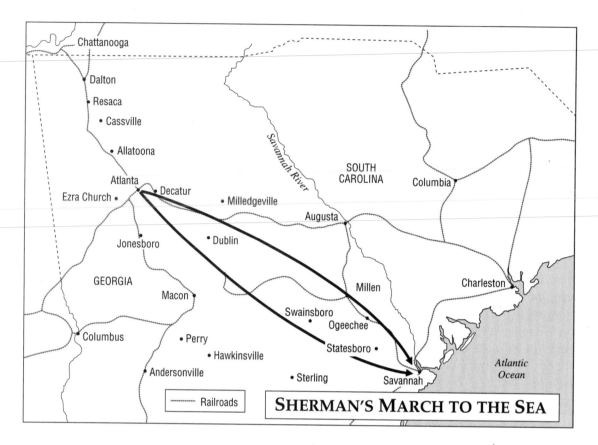

SHERMAN'S MARCH TO THE SEA

Chattanooga
Dalton
Resaca
Cassville
Allatoona
Atlanta • Decatur
Ezra Church
Milledgeville
Jonesboro
Dublin
GEORGIA
Macon
Augusta
SOUTH CAROLINA
Columbia
Charleston
Millen
Swainsboro
Ogeechee
Columbus
Perry
Hawkinsville
Statesboro
Savannah
Andersonville
Sterling
Savannah River
Atlantic Ocean

·········· Railroads

aid the Confederate war effort. The Federals took food, clothing, and weapons, and they burned houses and barns and killed livestock. They also freed slaves, who then joined the marching column.

Sherman's army cut a sixty-mile-wide path of destruction that stretched the three hundred miles to Savannah; Sherman later estimated that his army did 100 million dollars' worth of damage, leaving nothing for either the military or the civilian population. Sherman justified his actions to Grant, saying, "We cannot change the hearts of the people of the South, but we can make war so terrible that they will realize the fact that however brave and gallant and devoted to their country, still they are mortal and should exhaust all peaceful remedies before they fly to war."[56]

On December 10, Sherman reached Savannah, which he surrounded. Eleven days later, the Confederate garrison fled rather than surrender, and Sherman occupied the city.

The Confederacy's days were clearly numbered. As the new year dawned, Sherman would turn north to the Carolinas, and Grant would continue pushing hard at Petersburg.

8 1865: Victory and Defeat

By early 1865, the war was almost over. As Catton observes:

> It had been going on for nearly four years, and there would be about four more months of it. . . . There would be more graves to dig, and when there was time there would be thin bugle calls to lie in the still air while a handful of dust drifted down on a blanketed form. . . . A little more killing, a little more marching and burning and breaking and smashing, and then it would be ended.[57]

SLAVERY'S END

The war was not the only thing coming to an end in 1865. During the previous year, both Lincoln and congressional Republicans began to push for a thirteenth constitutional amendment that would abolish slavery. The president worried that, when the war was over, slavery could be renewed in the Southern states. Furthermore, the Emancipation Proclamation had not applied to the loyalist slave states, where slavery continued. Thus, Lincoln wanted to change the Constitution to end slavery completely in the United States.

By mid-1864, the Senate had ratified the Thirteenth Amendment, but the House was slow in its deliberations. Finally, on January 31, 1865, the House, voting before a huge audience of both whites and blacks, men and women, ratified the Thirteenth Amendment. The audience exploded in cheers and clapping. Outside, cannons fired a hundred-gun salute, people hugged each other in the street, and a brass band led a crowd to the White House lawn, where Lincoln praised Congress for its great moral victory.

SLIPPING AWAY

There was no celebration in the streets of Richmond that winter, for only diehard Southern separatists still thought a Confederate victory possible. Among these dedicated nationalists was Jefferson Davis, who in February gave a rousing speech. In it, says historian William C. Davis, he proclaimed that, "if only the men of the Confederacy would rush to the armies, he promised great victories in the field. . . . Davis even predicted that before the end of June, the North would come to him asking for peace."[58]

But the truth was that Southern men were not joining the armies. Indeed, they

Lincoln and members of his cabinet sign the Emancipation Proclamation, which would lead to the ratification of the Thirteenth Amendment in 1865.

were doing just the opposite. Desertion was draining the Confederate forces, particularly the Army of Northern Virginia. Scores deserted Lee every day, and during one ten-day period, more than a thousand men slipped away from Petersburg. The Confederates were growing desperately short of soldiers, not to mention food, clothing, weapons, and ammunition.

MARCHING THROUGH SOUTH CAROLINA

On February 1, Sherman began a new march that would take him north into the Carolinas. As with his march to the sea in Georgia, he intended to wage total war, particularly in South Carolina. Sherman and his men saw their planned destruction as a punishment of South Carolina, which as the first state to secede was the birthplace of the Confederacy and the

home of rebellion. As one Union soldier put it, "She [South Carolina] sowed the wind. She soon shall reap the whirlwind. She will yet weep tears of blood for her folly. . . . Well may she tremble."[59]

There was almost no Confederate resistance to the Union army or to the devastation it wrought. The destruction was far worse than in Georgia, as the Federals made no distinction between civilian and military property. Few houses remained unburned in their wake; nothing remained unlooted. On February 17, Sherman reached Columbia, the state capital, and burned it to the ground. The next day, the Federal navy captured Charleston, where the war's first shot was fired.

A MEETING IN NORTH CAROLINA

Lee was now general in chief of the Confederate army, his appointment having been confirmed in January. Upon news of Sherman's entry into South Carolina, Lee ordered Joseph Johnston to North Carolina with whatever troops could be mustered. Once in North Carolina, Johnston was to do his best to stop Sherman, who entered the state in early March.

Johnston's army numbered no more than twenty-one thousand, against more than five times that many Federals. At Bentonville, North Carolina, Johnston's small force battled Sherman for three days, March 19 through 21. But in the end, the Confederates had to fall back or be crushed. Johnston felt his only hope was for Lee to break out of Petersburg so the two commands could be united.

NOVELTY ITEMS

In the following account from Hardtack and Coffee, *quoted in* The Union Reader, *edited by Richard B. Harwell, former Union soldier John D. Billings described some of the useless merchandise peddled to Civil War soldiers:*

"Some of the inventions which I shall refer to were impractical, and had only a brief existence. . . . One of the first products . . . was a combination *knife-fork-and-spoon* arrangement. . . . Of course every man must have one. So much convenience in so small a compass [space], must be taken advantage of. . . . But I doubt whether this invention, on the average, ever got beyond the first camp in active service.

I still have in my possession the remnants of a *water-filterer.* . . . There was a metallic mouth-piece at one end of a small . . . tube, which latter was about fifteen inches long. At the other end of the tube was a suction-chamber, an inch long by a half-inch in diameter with the end perforated [pierced], and containing a piece of hocking [coarse wool] as a filter. . . . It is possible that I used this instrument half a dozen times. . . . I remember another filterer, somewhat simpler. . . . Neither of these was ever of any practical value. . . .

There were a good many men who preferred to be *live* heroes. . . . Well the iron tailors saw and appreciated the situation . . . of these men, and came to the rescue with a vest of steel armor. . . . Their owners were subjected to such a storm of ridicule that they could not bear up under it . . . ; so that it . . . the vest . . . adding no small weight to . . . [an] already too heavy burden was in many cases left behind."

AT PETERSBURG

Lee also thought the Confederacy's only hope was to combine his army with Johnston's. So, on March 25, in a desperate bid to break the Army of Northern Virginia free of Petersburg, Lee attacked the Union's Fort Stedman, just east of the city. The rebels managed to capture several artillery pieces and a half-mile of Federal trenches. They seemed on the verge of making it through the Union line when a massive counterattack sent them reeling back to Petersburg. It was Lee's last offensive.

A few days later, Grant dispatched Sheridan's cavalry and a corps of infantry to attack George Pickett's troops at Five Forks, southwest of Petersburg. In a two-day battle, beginning March 31, the Federals and Confederates struggled, but Sheridan finally crushed Pickett's command. The next day, Grant ordered a full assault by the entire Union line, which hit and broke through the Confederate defenses.

THE FALL OF RICHMOND

Petersburg was taken, and, by the afternoon of April 1, Union soldiers began pushing toward Richmond. The Army of Northern Virginia fought hard until dark and then retreated, passing quickly through Richmond without stopping. When Federal troops reached the Confederate capital the next morning, they met almost no resistance.

By the time the Federals arrived, Davis and the rest of the Confederate government had fled. Before the Confederate officials left, though, they set much of the city ablaze in an attempt to destroy government records.

Mobs of the city poor looted the burning city. One Southerner left this description of his final impressions of the fallen Southern capital:

> The great crowd as we soon saw, were . . . pillaging the burning city. . . . The roaring and crackling of the burning houses, the trampling and snorting of our horses over the paved streets, . . . wild sounds . . . through the cloud of smoke that hung like a pall . . . made a scene that beggars [defies] description. . . . The saddest of many of the sad sights of war—a city undergoing pillage at the hands of its own mob, while the standards of an empire were being taken from its capital, and the tramp of a victorious enemy could be heard at its gates.[60]

LEE'S LAST CAMPAIGN

Lee would not yet admit defeat, however. Instead, he planned to move his ragged and exhausted thirty-five thousand soldiers as rapidly as possible to Danville, Virginia, on the North Carolina border, and link up with Johnston. Lee hoped that, by merging the two armies, he would have a sufficiently large force to continue fighting.

First, however, the Army of Northern Virginia needed food. Thus, the Army of Northern Virginia made for Amelia Court House, where they were supposed to meet a supply train. All they found were empty tracks. Through some mistake, the train had kept on to Richmond and been captured.

His army starving, Lee scoured the countryside for food. Little was to be

LEE URGES PEACE

In a last letter to Jefferson Davis, written after the surrender at Appomattox and reprinted in The Wartime Papers of R.E. Lee, *Lee defends his actions and explains why he feels further resistance is futile:*

"The apprehensions that I expressed during the winter . . . have been realized. The operations that occurred while the troops were entrenched in front of Richmond and Petersburg . . . were feeble; and a want of confidence seemed to possess officers and men. This condition . . . was produced by the state of feeling in the country, and in the communications received by the men from their homes, urging their return and the abandonment of the field. . . . On the morning of 2d April, when our lines . . . were assaulted, the resistance was not effectual: several points were penetrated and large captures made. At the commencement of the withdrawal of the army . . . it began to disintegrate, and straggling from the ranks increased up to the surrender. . . . From what I have seen and learned, I believe an army cannot be organized or supported in Virginia, and as far as I know the condition of affairs, the country east of the Mississippi is morally and physically unable to maintain a contest unaided with any hope of ultimate success. A partisan [guerilla] war may be continued, and hostilities protracted, causing individual suffering and the devastation of the country, but I see no prospect by that means of achieving a separate independence. . . . To save useless . . . blood[shed], I would recommend measures be taken for suspension of hostilities and the restoration of peace."

found, and Lee started west, hoping to reach the town of Farmville, where he could receive supplies sent from Lynchburg, Virginia.

The search for food had wasted valuable time, and by the time Lee headed toward Farmville, the Federals were both in front of the Army of Northern Virginia and behind. On April 6, units of the Army of the Potomac caught up to Lee's rear guard and launched a shattering attack that left seven thousand dead or wounded Confederates.

At Farmville, Lee obtained rations for his troops but found his way south to North Carolina blocked. He therefore continued west, hoping to lose the Union troops in the mountains. Grant and his men kept close to the Confederates, and on April 8, near the town of Appomattox

Richmond, Virginia, smolders in the aftermath of blazes set by Confederate government officials fleeing the advancing Union army.

Courthouse in central Virginia, Lee found himself surrounded by overwhelming numbers of Federals.

LEE SURRENDERS

On the afternoon of April 9, Lee met with Grant to negotiate a surrender. Grant offered Lee very generous surrender terms. Besides the yielding up of weapons and ammunition, all that was required was that each Confederate soldier swear never again to take up arms against the United States. In exchange, every Confederate was then free to go home. There would be no prison, no trials, no executions. Additionally, those with horses or mules could keep them for use in spring plowing, and officers could retain their side arms. These would be the terms offered all Confederate commanders. Lee agreed.

Then, writes Leckie, after the signing of the surrender agreement:

Lee arose and shook hands with Grant. . . . On the porch of the [house where the negotiations had taken place] . . . he paused to draw on his gauntlets [gloves]. He gazed sadly toward the hillside where his little army lay, faithful and fearless to the last. Twice with slow and savage ruefulness, Lee drove his fist into his palm, then crying for Traveller [his horse] in a hoarse and choking voice, he mounted and rode out of sight.[61]

Four days later, the soldiers of the Army of Northern Virginia assembled for the last time, stacked their arms and battle flags, and went home.

PLANS FOR THE SOUTH

With the war winding down, the question of how the reconstruction, that is, reintegration, of the South should be handled brought the president and congressional Republicans into conflict. For Lincoln, ever practical and flexible, it was enough if Southerners pledged loyalty to the Union and freed their slaves. For congressional Republicans, often extreme in their beliefs, what was required was a complete overhaul of Southern society and politics.

It was the issue of reconstruction that Lincoln addressed on March 4 in his second inaugural address. The president urged his listeners and the nation to act

SURRENDER AT APPOMATTOX

On April 9, 1865, Robert E. Lee surrendered his army to Ulysses S. Grant at the town of Appomattox Courthouse, Virginia. Confederate colonel Charles Marshall left the following account, found in The Civil War Archive, *edited by Henry Steele Commager:*

"In about an hour we heard horses, and the first thing I knew General Grant walked into the room. There was with him General Sheridan . . . and quite a number of other officers. . . .

General Lee was standing at the end of the room opposite the door when General Grant walked in. General Grant had on . . . a loose fatigue coat, but he had no side arms. He looked as though he had had a pretty hard time. He had been riding and his clothes were somewhat dusty and a little soiled. He walked up to General Lee and Lee recognized him at once. . . . General Grant greeted him in the most cordial manner, and talked about the weather and other things in a very friendly manner. . . .

General Grant wrote the terms and conditions of surrender on . . . a paper that makes a copy at the same time as the note is written. . . . [Lee] read it over. . . . "I accept these terms.""

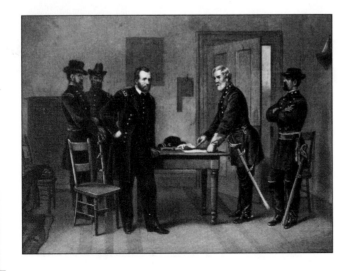

General Robert E. Lee (right) surrenders to General Ulysses S. Grant at Appomattox Courthouse, Virginia.

"with malice toward none; with charity for all, with firmness in the right, as God gives us to see the right."[62] The North was not to seek revenge on the South. However, as scholar Phillip Shaw Paludan points out, "Lincoln was not implying that the Union should forgive and forget; he was not urging that the . . . [South] be welcomed back without question, without stipulations, and without judgment."[63]

TOUR OF RICHMOND

On April 4, exactly one month after his inauguration, Lincoln visited Richmond to see the fallen Confederate capital for himself. Surrounded by only ten sailors, Lincoln wandered the streets; at one point he even sat in Jefferson Davis's chair in the Confederate executive mansion. The president soon found himself surrounded by former slaves, overjoyed to see the man who had spearheaded their liberation. The few of Richmond's white citizens who were on the street said and did nothing as the presidential party passed.

On April 11, a few days after Lincoln returned to Washington, the Northern capital celebrated Lee's surrender, for which a five-hundred-gun salute was fired. Crowds swarmed the streets, singing and shouting. People gathered outside the White House to hear Lincoln talk about the consequences of the war and about his hope that African American men would soon be granted the vote.

CONSPIRACY

One in the crowd, an actor, a Maryland native, and a Confederate sympathizer,

John Wilkes Booth (top, left) and other conspirators against Lincoln are shown in this photograph.

John Wilkes Booth, was enraged by the speech, particularly the idea of black citizenship. He swore to kill the president.

Throughout the winter of 1864–1865, Booth had gathered together a band of misfits with the idea of kidnapping Lincoln and taking him to Richmond. Nothing came of the plan, but now the actor enlisted several of his former conspirators in his assassination plan. His target was not only Lincoln, but also Vice President Andrew Johnson and Secretary of State Seward.

Booth soon discovered that Lincoln would be attending an April 14 performance of the popular play Our American

DEATH SCENE

U.S. Secretary of the Navy Gideon Welles witnessed the death of Abraham Lincoln and left the following description in his diary, excerpted in Fifty Basic Civil War Documents, *edited by Henry Steele Commager:*

"The giant sufferer lay extended diagonally across the bed, which was not long enough for him. He had been stripped of his clothes. His large arms, which were occasionally exposed, were of a size which one could scarce have expected from his spare [thin] appearance. His slow, full respiration lifted the clothes [sheets] with each breath that he took. His features were calm and striking. I had never seen them appear to better advantage than . . . for the first hour that I was there. After that, his right eye began to swell and that part of his face became discolored. . . .

A double guard was stationed at the door and on the sidewalk, to repress [control] the crowd, which was of course highly excited and anxious. The room was small and overcrowded. The surgeons and members of the Cabinet were as many as should have been in the room, but there were many more, and the hall and other rooms in the . . . house were full. One of these rooms was occupied by Mrs. Lincoln and her attendants. . . . About once an hour Mrs. Lincoln would repair [come] to the bedside of her dying husband and with lamentations and tears remain until overcome by emotion. . . .

A little before seven [a.m.], I went into the room where the dying President was rapidly drawing near the closing moments. His wife soon after made her last visit to him. The death-struggle had begun. . . . The respiration of the President became suspended at intervals, and at last entirely ceased."

The sixteenth president, Abraham Lincoln, was assassinated by John Wilkes Booth.

Cousin at Washington's Ford's Theater. That night, Booth crept into Lincoln's box and shot the president through the head. The actor then leaped to the stage, breaking his leg and shouting the motto of the state of Virginia, "Sic semper tyrannis" ("Thus always to tyrants").

THE DEATH OF LINCOLN

Booth's bullet did not kill Lincoln outright, and the president was carried to a house across the street. There, at 7:22 a.m. the next day, he died, never having regained consciousness. Three hours later, Andrew Johnson was sworn in as president of the United States.

The news of Lincoln's death ripped through the nation and the Northern armies. Northern joy turned to anguish. Leckie writes:

> The assassination of Abraham Lincoln stunned the Union as had no other event in the young nation's eighty-nine-year history. It was as though the shock waves of a moral earthquake were rolling across the country. [Both] admirers and . . . critics who had ridiculed the president as a "gorilla tyrant" or denounced him as a stupid, inept incompetent or damned him as a dictator and an enemy of liberty . . . lamented his murder with deep and moving grief.[64]

THE END OF THE CONSPIRACY

Of Johnson and Seward, only the secretary of state was attacked. Johnson was not approached at all; his assassin lost his nerve at the last minute. Seward survived despite several stab wounds.

Booth, whose leg had been set by Dr. Samuel Mudd, a Confederate supporter, was cornered by Union soldiers in a northern Virginia barn on April 26. When called upon to surrender, Booth refused, and the soldiers set the barn on fire. A shot then rang out, and Booth fell dead. The origin of the gunshot, whether from one of the soldiers or from Booth himself, is still unknown.

Seven people, including Mudd and the mother of one of the conspirators, Mary Surratt, were arrested for the assassination of Lincoln and tried before a military court. Surratt, whose son John had fled to Canada and would later claim to have had nothing to do with the assassination, was another Confederate sympathizer. It was in her Washington boarding house that some of the planning had occurred. Whether she or Mudd had a hand in the assassination, or even knew about it, is still a matter of debate, but in any case, all were found guilty. Mary Surratt and three others were hanged on July 7, and the remaining three were imprisoned. Mudd was pardoned by Andrew Johnson in 1868.

THE FINAL DAYS OF WAR

As the North mourned the death of Lincoln, Union troops completed the destruction of the Confederacy. On April 14, Federal soldiers celebrated the recapture of Fort Sumter, evacuated by the Union four years before. In North Carolina, on April 26, Sherman accepted Johnston's surrender. And, two weeks later,

ANDERSONVILLE

By the end of the war, both sides had thousands of prisoners of war stashed away in prison camps. Although conditions were not good in any of the camps, by far the worst were found in the Confederate prison Andersonville in Georgia, as seen in this deposition by Union private Prescott Tracy, reprinted in The Union Reader, *edited by Richard B. Harwell:*

"On entering the Stockade Prison, we found it crowded with twenty-eight thousand of our fellow soldiers. By *crowded*, I mean it was difficult to move in any direction without jostling and being jostled. . . .

Through the ground . . . creeps a stream . . . , filled with refuse wood, stumps and debris of the camp. Before entering the enclosure, the stream, or more properly sewer, passes through the camp of the guards, receiving from this source . . . a large amount of the vilest material. . . . This was our only drinking and cooking water. . . .

Our only shelter from the sun and the rain . . . was what we could make by stretching over us our coats or scraps of blankets. . . .

The proportion of deaths from *starvation*, not including those consequent to the diseases originating in the character and limited quantity of food, such as diarrhoea, dysentery, and scurvy, . . . were scores every month. We could at any time point out many for whom such a fate was inevitable, as they lay or feebly walked, mere skeletons. . . . The ration, in quantity, was perhaps barely sufficient to sustain life, and the cases of starvation were generally those whose stomachs could not retain what had become entirely indigestible.

For a man to find, on waking, that his comrade by his side was dead, was an occurrence too common to be noted."

on May 10, in Georgia, Federal cavalry captured Jefferson Davis, who was hustled off to prison at Fort Monroe, Virginia.

One final battle was fought. On May 13, Union colonel Theodore H. Barrett attacked a Confederate unit at Palmito Ranch, near Brownsville, Texas. Barrett lost both the fight and some thirty soldiers. Two weeks later, on May 26, Union general Edward Canby accepted E. Kirby Smith's surrender of the last active Confederate troops. The war was over.

War's Aftermath

The Union victory was complete, and the Southern states were once more a part of the United States. Yet it was not the United States of the prewar years. For out of the Civil War had come a new country, one dominated by Northern values. As McPherson points out, "The war tipped the sectional balance of power in favor of the North."[65] Over the next century, the United States, both North and South, would become a nation of industry, commerce, and cities.

It would be Northern politicians who would lead the country now. Before the war, most of the presidents were Southerners and slaveholders, as were the speakers of the House, presidents pro tem of the Senate, and Supreme Court justices. Afterward, for the next half-century, the South provided only one president, Woodrow Wilson; one speaker; no presidents pro tem; and only five of twenty-six justices. And the dominant party would be the Republican: Between 1861 and 1933, all but three presidents were Republicans.

LIFE AFTER THE WAR

But in the late spring of 1865, what was important for the moment was that the killing was done and the dying over. On May 23–24, before disbanding the armies that had brought victory, the Johnson administration held the Grand Review, in which a quarter of a million Union soldiers paraded through the streets of Washington in a huge celebration. Then the men went home to reenter civilian life.

Many of the top Union generals stayed in the army. Grant remained army commander until 1868 when he ran successfully for president. His two terms in office, however, were marked by scandal and corruption, although he himself was never accused of wrongdoing. Grant's later life was plagued by financial difficulties, which prompted him to write his memoirs. Finished just days before his death from cancer in 1885, the book earned his family almost a half-million dollars.

In 1869, Sherman replaced Grant as general in chief of the army, a position he held until his retirement in 1883. He retreated to write his own memoirs of the war and, although persistently asked to run for president, staunchly refused, saying that "the more I see of politicians the more averse [reluctant] I become to be one of them."[66] Sherman died in 1891.

For the former Confederates, everything was different. Scholar Erik Bruun writes:

> At the conclusion of the Civil War, much of the South was in a state of ruin and confusion: cities were devastated, towns sacked [looted], fields lay fallow [unplanted], and the economy in shambles. . . . For millions of people, the main goal in the immediate months after the war was survival.[67]

Even many of the wealthy—at least temporarily—were impoverished. One former Confederate officer sold apple pies baked by his wife, another peddled tea and molasses to his former slaves, and still another caught and sold fish and oysters. An armless veteran had his wife hitch him to a plow so that his fields could be planted. Everyone, white and black, struggled for years to restore both the land and the economy.

HOW THEY FARED

The South was occupied by Federal troops for the next twelve years, but there was no vengeance taken by the winners. Few former Confederates served jail terms, and only one was executed.

Jefferson Davis spent two years in prison facing charges of treason, but he was never tried. After his release, he stayed in Canada before returning to Mississippi, where he wrote *The Rise and Fall of the Confederate Government* before his death in 1889. He never tried to have his U.S. citizenship restored, preferring to remain a firm Confederate nationalist.

Lee became president of Washington University (later renamed Washington and Lee) in Lexington, Virginia, where he remained until his death in 1870. Unlike many of the other generals, both Federal and Confederate, he never wrote about his war experiences, although privately he believed that he had fought for a just cause. Following the advice he gave

The victorious Union army parades through Washington in the Grand Review of troops on May 23, 1865.

others, Lee took the loyalty oath and applied for restoration of his U.S. citizenship. However, his appeal was misplaced and not rediscovered until the 1970s. A special act, passed by Congress and signed by President Gerald Ford in 1975, finally restored Lee's citizenship posthumously.

Many of the other high-ranking officers and officials of the Confederacy eventually became businessmen or entered local and state politics. A few, such as James Longstreet and John Singleton Mosby (a noted Confederate guerrilla), found they shared similar political views with their one-time enemies and horrified their compatriots by becoming Republicans and supporters of Ulysses S. Grant, who named Longstreet as U.S. minister to Turkey and Mosby U.S. consul in Hong Kong. Longstreet, as one of Lee's officers, was seen by Southerners as the worst renegade, and Longstreet's former Confederate army mate Jubal Early vilified him, even going so far as to blame Longstreet for the loss at Gettysburg. Early claimed that Longstreet had acted with deliberate slowness in response to Lee's orders because he had disagreed with the latter's overall strategy.

AFRICAN AMERICANS

For the 3.5 million African Americans in the South, the future seemed bright. Two more constitutional amendments, the Fourteenth (1868) and Fifteenth (1870), gave blacks the right to vote and guaranteed their civil liberties. And during Reconstruction, the period of Federal oversight of the South that lasted from 1867 to 1877, African Americans seemed poised to enjoy their citizenship: They voted, held office, set up schools and businesses, and owned property.

However, there were many forces arrayed against Southern blacks. President Andrew Johnson, a pro-Unionist Southerner, balked at protecting the civil rights of African Americans. Indeed, his relations with Congress over Reconstruction policy became so bad that, in 1868, he was impeached and came within one vote of being removed from office.

Soldiers stand at attention for the execution of Henry Wirz, the only convicted war criminal of the Civil War.

Nathan Bedford Forrest organized and led the Ku Klux Klan.

Southern whites were angered over what they saw as preferential treatment of the former slaves. Such white-supremacy organizations as the Ku Klux Klan, one of whose leaders was one-time Confederate cavalry leader Nathan Bedford Forrest, and the Knights of the White Camellia spread terror, beating and killing blacks and their white supporters.

With the end of Reconstruction, all efforts at fair treatment for African Americans in the South disappeared. White communities required literacy tests and the payment of taxes for voter registration, thus denying blacks their right to vote. Jim Crow laws required racial segregation of all public places—schools,

parks, rest rooms, even water fountains. African Americans would not begin to regain their lost rights until the Civil Rights movement of the 1950s and 1960s.

A Road and a Testing

As bad as these restrictions were for black Americans, eventually they would be overturned, in large part because of the Civil War. Leckie writes:

> So slavery was succeeded by [Southern] segregation . . . , and in the teeming black slums of the Northern cities by the same . . . if not authorized injustices. Yet from prolonged pain and great convulsions come new perceptions and new directions. The Civil War indeed shocked the American nation. . . . At first there may have been barely more than glimpses of what social good might come from all this agony. They would grow into true visions and purpose while over the decades Southerners and Northerners ceased to despise each other. . . . After it [the Civil War] the United States truly became "one nation indivisible" and the American ideal of "freedom and justice for all" was put on the road toward reality.[68]

As he made clear in the Gettysburg Address, Abraham Lincoln saw the Civil War as a testing to see if a "government of the people, by the people, for the people shall not perish from the earth." The Union victory ensured that the United States would survive intact and that the nation also achieved what Lincoln called "a new birth of freedom."[69]

Notes

Introduction: The Great Conflict

1. James M. McPherson, *Battle Cry of Freedom: The Civil War Era*. Oxford: Oxford University Press, 1988, pp. viii–ix.

2. McPherson, *Battle Cry of Freedom*, p. x.

3. Russell F. Weigley, *A Great Civil War: A Military and Political History, 1861–1865*. Bloomington: Indiana University Press, 2000, p. xviii.

4. Robert Leckie, *None Died in Vain: The Saga of the American Civil War*. New York: Harper-Collins, 1990, p. 657.

Chapter 1: The Road to War

5. Weigley, *A Great Civil War*, p. xxvii.

6. Emory M. Thomas, *The Confederate Nation: 1861–1865*. New York: History Book Club, 1979, p. 105.

7. Steven E. Woodworth, *Cultures in Conflict: The American Civil War*. Westport, CT: Greenwood Press, 2000, p. 32.

8. Quoted in Mark E. Neely Jr. *The Last Best Hope of Earth: Abraham Lincoln and the Promise of America*. Cambridge, MA: Harvard University Press, 1993, pp. 39–40.

9. Quoted in David Herbert Donald, *Lincoln*. New York: Simon and Schuster, 1995, p. 207.

10. Quoted in Frank Moore, ed., *The Rebellion Record: Supplement*. New York: G.P. Putnam, 1864, Document 147½.

11. William C. Davis, *"A Government of Our Own": The Making of the Confederacy*. New York: The Free Press, 1994, p. 87.

Chapter 2: 1861: Opening Shots

12. Bruce Catton, *The Centennial History of the Civil War*. Vol. 1: *The Coming Fury*. New York: Doubleday, 1961, p. 201.

13. Quoted in Catton, *The Coming Fury*, p. 331.

14. Quoted in McPherson, *Battle Cry of Freedom*, p. 337.

15. Joseph L. Harsh, *Confederate Tide Rising: Robert E. Lee and the Making of Southern Strategy, 1861–1862*. Kent, OH: Kent State University Press, 1998, pp. 9–10.

16. Richard Wheeler, *A Rising Thunder: From Lincoln's Election to the Battle of Bull Run: An Eyewitness History*. New York: HarperCollins, 1994, p. 236.

17. Quoted in William C. Davis, *Battle at Bull Run: A History of the First Major Campaign of the Civil War*. New York: Doubleday, 1977, p. 197.

18. Quoted in James I. Robertson Jr., *Stonewall Jackson: The Man, the Soldier, the Legend*. New York: Macmillan, 1997, p. xiii.

19. Davis, *Battle at Bull Run*, p. 255.

Chapter 3: 1862: The Eastern War

20. Catton, *The Coming Fury*, pp. 404, 407.

21. William C. Davis, *Jefferson Davis: The Man and His Hour*. Baton Rouge: Louisiana State University Press, 1991, p. 388.

22. Quoted in Emory M. Thomas, *Robert E. Lee: A Biography*. New York: Norton, 1995, p. 226.

23. Robertson, *Stonewall Jackson*, p. 510.

24. Quoted in Shelby Foote, *The Civil War: A Narrative: Fort Sumter to Perryville*. New York: Vintage Books, 1958, p. 662.

25. McPherson, *Battle Cry of Freedom*, p. 558.

26. Quoted in Bruce Catton, *The Army of the Potomac: Mr. Lincoln's Army*. Revised Edition. Garden City, NY: Doubleday, 1962, p. 322.

27. Richard Wheeler, *Lee's Terrible Swift Sword: From Antietam to Chancellorsville: An Eyewitness History.* New York: HarperCollins, 1992, p. 3.

Chapter 4: 1862: The Western War

28. Bruce Catton, *The Centennial History of the Civil War.* Vol. 2: *Terrible Swift Sword.* New York: Doubleday, 1963, pp. 28–29.

29. Ulysses S. Grant, *Personal Memoirs of U. S. Grant.* Lincoln: University of Nebraska Press, 1885, p. 164.

30. Quoted in Gene Smith, *Lee and Grant: A Dual Biography.* New York: McGraw-Hill, 1984, p. 122.

31. Ivan Musicant, *Divided Waters: The Naval History of the Civil War.* New York: Harper-Collins, 1995, p. 224.

32. Catton, *Terrible Swift Sword*, p. 375.

33. Foote, *Fort Sumter to Perryville*, p. 740.

34. William T. Sherman, *Memoirs of William T. Sherman by Himself.* Bloomington: Indiana University Press, 1875, p. 295.

Chapter 5: 1863: The Home Fronts

35. Quoted in Donald, *Lincoln*, p. 399.

36. Quoted in James M. McPherson, ed., *The Atlas of the Civil War.* New York: Macmillan, 1994, p. 95.

37. Neely, *The Last Best Hope of Earth*, p. 138.

38. Quoted in McPherson, *The Atlas of the Civil War*, p. 96.

39. Davis, *Jefferson Davis*, p. 389.

40. Thomas, *The Confederate Nation*, pp. 224–25.

41. Quoted in McPherson, *The Atlas of the Civil War*, p. 96.

Chapter 6: 1863: Turning Points

42. Thomas B. Buell, *The Warrior Generals: Combat Leadership in the Civil War.* New York: Crown, 1997, p. 215.

43. Robertson, *Stonewall Jackson*, p. 755.

44. Quoted in Richard Wheeler, ed., *Voices of the Civil War.* New York: Crowell, 1976, p. 278.

45. Quoted in Albert A. Nofi, *The Gettysburg Campaign: June–July 1863.* Revised Edition. Conshohocken, PA: Combined Books, 1993, pp. 173–75.

46. James Longstreet, *From Manassas to Appomattox: Memoirs of the Civil War in America.* Edited by James I. Robertson Jr. Bloomington: Indiana University Press, 1960, pp. 386–87.

47. Quoted in Nofi, *The Gettysburg Campaign*, p. 206.

48. Musicant, *Divided Waters*, p. 287.

49. Quoted in McPherson, *The Atlas of the Civil War*, p. 99.

50. Quoted in Nofi, *The Gettysburg Campaign*, p. 225.

Chapter 7: 1864: The War Continues

51. Geoffrey Perret, *Ulysses S. Grant: Soldier and President.* New York: Random House, 1997, p. 301.

52. Grant, *Personal Memoirs of U. S. Grant*, p. 503.

53. Allan Nevins, *The War for the Union.* Vol. 4: *The Organized War to Victory: 1864–1865.* New York: Scribner's, 1971, p. 45.

54. Quoted in Shelby Foote, *The Civil War: A Narrative: Red River to Appomattox.* New York: Vintage Books, 1974, p. 472.

55. Bruce Catton, *This Hallowed Ground: The Story of the Union Side of the Civil War.* New York: Doubleday, 1956, p. 353.

56. Quoted in Foote, *Fort Sumter to Perryville*, p. 801.

Chapter 8: 1865: Victory and Defeat

57. Catton, *This Hallowed Ground*, p. 370.

58. Davis, *Jefferson Davis*, p. 594.

59. Quoted in Michael Fellman, *Citizen Sherman: A Life of William Tecumseh Sherman*. New York: Random House, 1995, p. 222.

60. Quoted in Nevins, *The Organized War to Victory: 1864–1865*, p. 295.

61. Leckie, *None Died in Vain*, pp. 638–39.

62. Quoted in Donald, *Lincoln*, p. 567.

63. Phillip Shaw Paludan, *The Presidency of Abraham Lincoln*. Lawrence: University Press of Kansas, 1994, p. 304.

64. Leckie, *None Died in Vain*, p. 648.

Conclusion: War's Aftermath

65. McPherson, *The Atlas of the Civil War*, p. 214.

66. Quoted in Fellman, *Citizen Sherman*, p. 311.

67. Henry Steele Commager, ed., *The Civil War Archive: The History of the Civil War in Documents*. Revised and expanded by Erik Bruun. New York: Black Dog and Leventhal, 2000, p. 788.

68. Leckie, *None Died in Vain*, pp. 657–58.

69. Quoted in Neely, *The Last Best Hope of Earth*, p. 156.

For Further Reading

Books

Timothy L. Biel, *Life in the North During the Civil War.* San Diego: Lucent Books, 1997. Filled with photographs and eyewitness accounts, this study looks at the effects of the war upon the North, and examines the diverse reactions to and opinions about the conflict of the people of the Union.

Jack Coggins, *Arms and Equipment of the Civil War.* New York: Fairfax Press, 1962. Provides good, detailed information on Union and Confederate weapons, uniforms, and equipment, as well as explaining the organization and duties of the infantry, cavalry, signal corps, and the engineers. The text is highlighted by the author's vivid and historically accurate illustrations.

James A. Corrick, *The Battle of Gettysburg.* San Diego: Lucent Books, 1996. Supported by reports of participants, maps, and period photographs, this detailed account describes the events that led up to this conflict, the battle itself, and the aftermath. Additional material includes a time line and a reading list.

———, *The Civil War: Life Among the Soldiers and Cavalry.* San Diego: Lucent Books, 2000. Through firsthand accounts, details the enlistment, training, and equipping of soldiers and cavalry on both sides, as well as describing the activities in camp, on the march, and in battle.

Stephen Crane, *The Red Badge of Courage.* New York: Bantam Classics, 1981. This classic novel presents a graphic and realistic picture of the Civil War battlefield. In clear, vivid words, the author makes a young recruit's first day in combat come alive.

Stephen Currie, *Slavery.* San Diego: Greenhaven Press, 1998. Airs the pros and cons of the nineteenth-century debate on slavery, letting those involved speak for themselves. Includes a bibliography, statistics, and a list of important documents.

William Dudley, ed., *The Civil War: Opposing Viewpoints.* San Diego: Greenhaven Press, 1995. A collection of Civil War writings, which present in chronological order and in pro/con format the issues that led up to the war and that led to internal divisions within North and South during the conflict.

David Haugen and Lori Shein, *The Civil War.* San Diego: Greenhaven Press, 1998. Presents opposing viewpoints on the important issues of the war, from slavery to secession to the role of black soldiers. Relies on quotations from both participants and later historians, and includes a bibliography and list of important documents.

Philip Katcher, *The Civil War Source Book.* New York: Facts On File, 1992. Ten sections and several hundred entries furnish worthwhile information on the

Union and Confederate armies. Covered are uniforms, weapons, camp life, discipline, prisons, battlefield medicine, and even salaries, to name a few. There are also biographies of major figures, photographs, maps, a glossary, and a bibliography.

Stephen R. Lilley, *Fighters Against American Slavery*. San Diego: Lucent Books, 1999. Through biographical sketches of important abolitionists, such as William Lloyd Garrison and Frederick Douglass, and other opponents of slavery, such as Nat Turner, the history of the running battle against slavery emerges. Supplemental material includes photographs, eyewitness accounts, and a reading list.

James P. Reger, *The Battle of Antietam*. San Diego: Lucent Books, 1997. Describes this campaign and the events surrounding it, as well as examining the battle's effects, particularly in convincing Lincoln to issue the Emancipation Proclamation. The text is accompanied by photographs, quotations, a time line, and a reading list.

———, *Civil War Generals of the Confederacy*. San Diego: Lucent Books, 1999. Individual biographies of such Confederate military leaders as Robert E. Lee, Jeb Stuart, and Stonewall Jackson reveal the virtues that brought them victory even though they were generally outnumbered. Supported by photographs, quotations, and a reading list.

———, *Life in the South During the Civil War*. San Diego: Lucent Books, 1997. Examines the way Southerners viewed the Civil War as an invasion and the Northern victory as the bitter end of their chosen way of life. The text is supported by many period photographs, quotations from the time, and a reading list.

Russell Roberts, *The Civil War: Lincoln and the Abolition of Slavery*. San Diego: Lucent Books, 2000. Explains how Lincoln, through a combination of patience, wisdom, and political savvy, convinced the American public that a major goal of the Civil War was to abolish slavery.

Stewart Sifakis, *Who Was Who in the Civil War*. New York: Facts On File, 1988. Provides much interesting and worthwhile information on some twenty-five hundred individuals who served the Union or the Confederacy.

Gail B. Stewart, *The Civil War: Weapons of War*. San Diego: Lucent Books, 2000. Describes the many weapons—rifles, cannons, torpedoes, ironclads, machine guns—how they were used, and the effect they had on victory and defeat in the war.

Thomas Streissguth, ed., *The Civil War: The North*. San Diego: Greenhaven Press, 2001.

———, ed., *The Civil War: The South*. San Diego: Greenhaven Press, 2001. Complementary volumes that tell the story of the Civil War through the letters, diaries, and reports of citizens and soldiers on both sides. Topics include the early Confederate victories, life in the armies, the role of black soldiers in the Union army, and life on the home fronts.

————, ed., *Slavery*. San Diego: Greenhaven Press, 2001. Collection that presents the history of slavery through personal accounts of slaves, slaveholders, abolitionists, and outside observers.

James Tackach, *The Emancipation Proclamation*. San Diego: Lucent Books, 1999. Quoting from abolitionist writings, Lincoln's speeches, and court rulings, fills in the background behind the proclamation. It then looks at the document's effect on the war and on American society.

Rafael Tilton, *Clara Barton*. San Diego: Lucent Books, 1995. A readable biography of the life of this famous Civil War nurse and her later role in founding the American Red Cross. Extensive quotations from the period and later, along with a time line of Barton's life and a reading list, add to the value of the text.

Diane Yancey, *The Civil War: Leaders of the North and South*. San Diego: Lucent Books, 2000. Informative sketches on the many leaders of the war, from abolitionists to politicians, military men to female soldiers and spies.

————, *The Civil War: Strategic Battles*. San Diego: Lucent Books, 2000. Examines the importance of improved weapons and strategy in several major battles of the war, including Fort Sumter, Antietam, Gettysburg, and Vicksburg.

————, *Civil War Generals of the Union*. San Diego: Lucent Books, 1999. Traces the lives of such Union commanders as Grant, McClellan, and Sherman, showing what qualities brought them success or failure. Many photographs and quotations round out the individual portraits.

Websites

The American Civil War, 2001 (www.homepages.dsu.edu). Several hundred links to Civil War sites listing information on battles, people, the Confederacy, weapons, and many other aspects of the war. There are several links to online reproductions of diaries and letters as well.

The Civil War, 2001 (www.militaryhistory-online.com). Provides articles, maps, and photographs of such battles as Antietam, Chancellorsville, Fredericksburg, and Gettysburg.

The Civil War as Photographed by Matthew Brady, 1999 (www.nara.gov). National Archive images of some of Matthew Brady's photographs taken during the Civil War, showing battlefields, camp life, hospitals, and prisoners.

TeachPDLaw's Research World: The Civil War, 2001 (www.members.aol.com). Provides useful and detailed information on the causes of the war, slavery, terminology, the Confederacy, currency, economics, civilian life, battles, medicine, flags, maps, military and civilian personnel, spies, women, music, art, and poetry.

TreasureNet Historical Image Collection, 2001 (www.treasurenet.com). Displays many period Civil War photographs: officers and enlisted men on both sides, prisons, camp life, naval vessels, and much more.

Works Consulted

Russell H. Beatie Jr., *Road to Manassas.* New York: Cooper Square, 1961. A solid study of the events that led up to the first major battle of the war.

Thomas B. Buell, *The Warrior Generals: Combat Leadership in the Civil War.* New York: Crown, 1997. An examination of the military skill possessed by both Union and Confederate generals.

Rice C. Bull, *Soldiering: The Civil War Diary of Rice C. Bull, 123rd New York Volunteer Infantry.* Ed. K. Jack Bauer. Novato, CA: Presidio Press, 1977. An informative day-to-day record of serving in the Army of the Potomac.

Bruce Catton, *The Army of the Potomac: Mr. Lincoln's Army.* Revised Edition. Garden City, NY: Doubleday, 1962. Tells the story of formation and early days of the Army of the Potomac.

————, *The Centennial History of the Civil War.* Vol. 1: *The Coming Fury.* New York: Doubleday, 1961.

————, *The Centennial History of the Civil War.* Vol. 2: *Terrible Swift Sword.* New York: Doubleday, 1963.

————, *The Centennial History of the Civil War.* Vol. 3: *Never Call Retreat.* New York: Doubleday, 1965. By an important Civil War historian, this classic study of the war is full of detail, analysis, and insight about causes, battles, and historical figures. Quotations from participants and excellent maps add to these volumes' usefulness.

————, *This Hallowed Ground: The Story of the Union Side of the Civil War.* New York: Doubleday, 1956. A good, readable, short history of the Union's struggles, written by a noted authority on the period.

Mary Chesnut, *A Diary from Dixie.* Eds. Isabella D. Martin and Myrta Lockett Avary. Gloucester, MA: Smith, 1905. An intimate and intriguing look at life in the Confederacy.

Henry Steele Commager, ed., *The Blue and the Gray: Two Volumes in One: The Story of the Civil War as Told by Participants.* New York: Fairfax Press, 1960. This excellent collection of original writings from the Civil War, complete with illustrations, is divided into sections, covering many topics, such as important campaigns and battles, camp life, prisons, and civilian reactions.

————, ed., *The Civil War Archive: The History of the Civil War in Documents.* Revised and expanded by Erik Bruun. New York: Black Dog and Leventhal, 2000. A massive collection of period pieces, covering every aspect of military and civilian life.

————, ed., *Fifty Basic Civil War Documents.* New York: Van Nostrand Reinhold, 1965. A useful compilation of writings from the period, including inaugural addresses, responses to the Emancipation Proclamation, battle reports, and newspaper articles and editorials.

William C. Davis, *Battle at Bull Run: A History of the First Major Campaign of the Civil War*. New York: Doubleday, 1977. This study, filled with useful maps, provides a detailed look at this first major battle of the war.

————, *"A Government of Our Own": The Making of the Confederacy*. New York: The Free Press, 1994. A well-known Civil War historian tells the story of the Confederate constitutional convention.

————, *Jefferson Davis: The Man and His Hour*. Baton Rouge: Louisiana State University Press, 1991. An excellent, well-written biography of the Confederate president.

David Herbert Donald, *Lincoln*. New York: Simon and Schuster, 1995. This recent Lincoln biography is readable and filled with useful information.

Jubal Anderson Early, *War Memoirs: Autobiographical Sketch and Narrative of the War between the States*. Ed. Frank E. Vandiver. Bloomington: Indiana University Press, 1960. An account of the Civil War, as told by one of Lee's trusted generals.

Michael Fellman, *Citizen Sherman: A Life of William Tecumseh Sherman*. New York: Random House, 1995. Well-received biography of one of the Union's most successful generals.

Philip S. Foner, ed., *The Life and Writings of Frederick Douglass*. New York: International Publishers, 1952. An informative discussion of Douglass, as well as a useful selection from this elegant and articulate abolitionist and former slave's writing.

Shelby Foote, *The Civil War: A Narrative: Fort Sumter to Perryville*. New York: Vintage Books, 1958.

————, *The Civil War: A Narrative: Fredericksburg to Meridian*. New York: Vintage Books, 1963.

————, *The Civil War: A Narrative: Red River to Appomattox*. New York: Vintage Books, 1974. This scholarly work is a thorough and elegantly written military history of the war. It covers in great detail and with considerable insight the various campaigns as well as the nature of the men who fought in them and the rigors and hardships they endured.

Douglas Southall Freeman, *Lee's Lieutenants: A Study in Command*. Ed. Stephen W. Sears. New York: Scribner, 1998. One of the best studies of the generals who served in the Army of Northern Virginia.

Ulysses S. Grant, *Personal Memoirs of U.S. Grant*. Lincoln: University of Nebraska Press, 1885. Much of this readable and thorough autobiography is devoted to Grant's wartime experiences.

Parthenia Hague, *A Blockaded Family: Life in Southern Alabama during the Civil*

War. Boston: Houghton Mifflin, 1888. A vivid first-hand account of the problems and hardships faced by Southern civilians.

Joseph L. Harsh, *Confederate Tide Rising: Robert E. Lee and the Making of Southern Strategy, 1861–1862.* Kent, OH: Kent State University Press, 1998. Describes in detail the evolution of Confederate strategy during the first two years of the war, with particular emphasis on the role of Lee in developing that strategy.

Richard B. Harwell, ed., *The Union Reader.* New York: Longmans, 1958. First-hand accounts by Union participants, beginning with Fort Sumter and ending with the final peace.

Hinton R. Helper, *The Impending Crisis of the South.* New York: A.B. Burdick, 1857. An intriguing examination by a Southerner of the economic problems of the prewar South and an impassioned plea for an end to slavery.

Philip Katcher, *The Army of Robert E. Lee.* London: Arms and Armour, 1994. A useful study of all aspects of the Army of Northern Virginia. Included are biographies of Lee and his generals and a look at the Confederate soldiers.

Robert Leckie, *None Died in Vain: The Saga of the American Civil War.* New York: HarperCollins, 1990. An even-handed history of the Civil War, of particular value for its examination of the issues that led up to the war.

Robert E. Lee, *The Wartime Papers of R.E. Lee.* Ed. Clifford Dowdey. Boston: Little, Brown, 1961. Brings together the orders, letters, and other writings of Lee during his service in the Confederate army.

James Longstreet, *From Manassas to Appomattox: Memoirs of the Civil War in America.* Ed. James I. Robertson Jr. Bloomington, IN: Indiana University Press, 1960. This important Confederate general provides an interesting account of his war experiences.

James M. McPherson, *Battle Cry of Freedom: The Civil War Era.* Oxford: Oxford University Press, 1988. An excellent one-volume history of the Civil War by a prominent historian of the period. Generous use of quotations strengthens the text.

———, ed., *The Atlas of the Civil War.* New York: Macmillan, 1994. An excellent resource that is filled with good, large maps in color and well-reproduced black-and-white photographs. Accompanying the maps are informative essays as well as reviews of the events of each year of the conflict.

Frank Moore, ed., *The Rebellion Record: Supplement.* New York: G.P. Putnam, 1864. An excellent collection of original writings from the period.

Ivan Musicant, *Divided Waters: The Naval History of the Civil War.* New York: HarperCollins, 1995. A well-researched history of the Union and Confederate navies, relating the story of the blockade, the river war, and the war at sea.

Mark E. Neely Jr., *The Last Best Hope of Earth: Abraham Lincoln and the Promise of America*. Cambridge, MA: Harvard University Press, 1993. An in-depth look at Lincoln's philosophy and his practical political skills.

Allan Nevins, *The War for the Union*. Vol. 4: *The Organized War to Victory: 1864–1865*. New York: Scribner's, 1971. The final volume of an important Civil War history, noted for its thoroughness and depth of analysis.

Albert A. Nofi, *The Gettysburg Campaign: June–July 1863*. Revised Edition. Conshohocken, PA: Combined Books, 1993. A good, general account of the Gettysburg campaign by a noted military historian. Its many useful facts are complemented by several detailed maps of the battle.

Phillip Shaw Paludan, *The Presidency of Abraham Lincoln*. Lawrence: University Press of Kansas, 1994. A year-by-year analysis of the Lincoln presidency.

Geoffrey Perret, *Ulysses S. Grant: Soldier and President*. New York: Random House, 1997. A good recent biography of the Union's supreme military commander, following him from West Point to his final days.

James I. Robertson Jr., *Stonewall Jackson: The Man, the Soldier, the Legend*. New York: Macmillan, 1997. This excellent and massive biography of one of the South's greatest generals uncovers the man behind the legend.

William T. Sherman, *Memoirs of William T. Sherman by Himself*. Bloomington: Indiana University Press, 1875. These recollections provide insight into this Union general's character and military philosophy.

Gene Smith, *Lee and Grant: A Dual Biography*. New York: McGraw-Hill, 1984. A good, general biography of the two most important Confederate and Federal generals.

Joseph E. Stevens, *1863: The Rebirth of a Nation*. New York: Bantam Books, 1999. Filled with maps and period photographs, this study provides a close look at the military and political events that determined the outcome of the war.

Annette Tapert, ed., *The Brothers' War: Civil War Letters to Their Loved Ones from the Blue and the Gray*. New York: Times Books, 1988. A collection of letters by both Union and Confederate soldiers that reveals how these men saw the war in which they fought. Photographs, which include some of the letter writers, illustrate the text.

Emory M. Thomas, *Bold Dragoon: The Life of J.E.B. Stuart*. Norman: University of Oklahoma Press, 1986. A good biography of this colorful Confederate cavalry leader.

———, *The Confederate Nation: 1861–1865*. New York: History Book Club, 1979. A noted historian's classic study of the formation, politics, and governmental operations of the Confederate States of America.

————, *Robert E. Lee: A Biography.* New York: Norton, 1995. An insightful look at the life and character of the South's foremost general. The text is filled with passages from Lee's battlefield reports and messages, as well as maps of his major battles.

Dorothy Denneen Volo and James M. Volo, *Daily Life in Civil War America.* Westport, CT: Greenwood Press, 1998. An informative examination of the everyday lives of both soldiers and civilians, North and South.

Russel F. Weigley, *A Great Civil War: A Military and Political History, 1861–1865.* Bloomington: Indiana University Press, 2000. Examines the tactics and strategies of both sides, as well as the ongoing political struggles in both North and South as the conflict progressed.

Richard Wheeler, *Lee's Terrible Swift Sword: From Antietam to Chancellorsville: An Eyewitness History.* New York: HarperCollins, 1992. Quotes liberally from letters, diaries, and newspaper and battle reports to tell the stories of Antietam, Fredericksburg, and Chancellorsville.

————, *A Rising Thunder: From Lincoln's Election to the Battle of Bull Run: An Eyewitness History.* New York: HarperCollins, 1994. Firsthand accounts of secession and the early months of the war.

————, ed., *Voices of the Civil War.* New York: Crowell, 1976. A good sampling of original writings. Selections are divided by campaign and battle.

Bell Irvin Wiley, *The Life of Billy Yank: The Common Soldier of the Union.* Indianapolis, IN: Bobbs-Merrill, 1952.

————, *The Life of Johnny Reb: The Common Soldier of the Confederacy.* Indianapolis, IN: Bobbs-Merrill, 1943. These two classic studies present in complete detail, often through the words of the men themselves, the lives of the Union and Confederate soldiers from enlistment to war's end. There are no better secondary sources for getting a feel for what it was like to soldier in the Civil War.

Frank Wilkeson, *Turned inside Out: Recollections of a Private Soldier in the Army of the Potomac.* Lincoln: University of Nebraska Press, 1886. A graphic, vivid, and gripping account of enlistment and service in the Federal army.

William J. Wood, *Civil War Generalship: The Art of Command.* Westport, CT: Praeger, 1997. A useful study of the strategic and tactical philosophy and conduct of several major Union and Confederate generals.

Steven E. Woodworth, *Cultures in Conflict: The American Civil War.* Westport, CT: Greenwood Press, 2000. Excerpts from letters and diaries reveal the emotions and thoughts of people, both North and South, prior to and during the war.

Index

Picture Credits

About the Author

James A. Corrick has been a professional writer and editor for twenty years and is the author of twenty-five books, as well as two hundred articles and short stories. His other books for Lucent are *The Early Middle Ages, The Late Middle Ages, The Battle of Gettysburg, The Byzantine Empire, The Renaissance, The Industrial Revolution, The Civil War: Life Among the Soldiers and Cavalry, The Louisiana Purchase, Life of a Medieval Knight*, and *The Inca*. Along with a Ph.D. in English, Corrick's academic background includes a graduate degree in the biological sciences. He has taught English, tutored minority students, edited magazines for the National Space Society, been a science writer for the Muscular Dystrophy Association, and edited and indexed books on history, economics, and literature for Columbia University Press, MIT Press, and others. Corrick and his wife live in Tucson, Arizona.